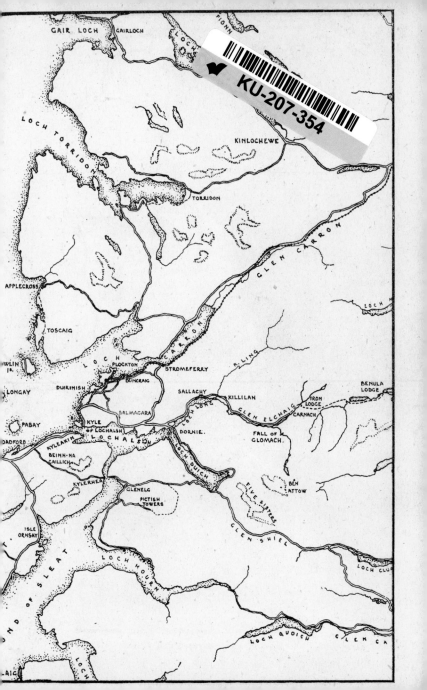

GATEWAY TO SKYE

ISLE OF SKYE AT SUNRISE, FROM KYLE OF LOCHALSH

GATEWAY TO SKYE

BY
DUNCAN MACPHERSON, F.S.A.Scot.

WITH ILLUSTRATIONS
AND A MAP

ENEAS MACKAY
STIRLING

First published, 1946

Printed at The Observer Press, Stirling, Scotland

IAN NEIL MACPHERSON

TO
NEIL

CONTENTS

LIST OF ILLUSTRATIONS

INTRODUCTION

WITH the first breath of Spring the tourist begins to find his way to our Highland glens ; and by the time Summer is here, hundreds are arriving daily. There are those who visit us, year after year, because of their great love for the Highlands and its inhabitants. Many are deeply interested in the life of the people, and to such in particular I am hopeful that this rambling record will be of interest.

It begins twenty-eight years ago, with my arrival at Kyle of Lochalsh one Spring afternoon. Behold me, then, a tall, miserably thin young man, setting foot on the rocky West in search of a livelihood, and even more vitally important, seeking after elusive health.

In the years that followed, amid the healing mountain breezes laden with the tang of the sea, I found the health I sought. I visited many of the historic places of Skye and the Western mainland. I saw the mountains over-hung by brooding clouds, and again in all the glory of a Summer morning or the heavenly beauty of a red-gold sunset. I found happiness in wife, family, and friends ; and if I did not discover wealth, I found a kindly banker in whose care it was a pleasure to place my overdraft.

I have set down here some of the lighter incidents of those years. These are not written in any spirit of criticism, but rather out of love for many worthy people whose words and actions it is a delight to recall.

DUNCAN MACPHERSON.

GLENQUITHEL,
KYLE OF LOCHALSH.

FOREWORD

ONE copy of *Gateway to Skye* was typed, illustrated, and bound in 1939, but publication had to be postponed because of the world upheaval which was emerging.

It was this typed copy which my son Neil read and re-read. He had lived through most of its scenes. He was with me as an infant in arms on my first visit to Elgol. In later years he was a frequent companion in my wanderings. Together we cycled along the hilly roads, trod by-paths and climbed mountain peaks or explored some dim sea cavern.

Skye, Ratagan, Glenelg, Glomach, Ach-na-hinich, Applecross, what memories! Neil loved the places and the people. He perceived kindliness and humour everywhere. On one of his last days at home on leave he turned to the pages of the *Gateway*. He saw no imperfections. May the reader be equally merciful!

D. M.

KYLE OF LOCHALSH,
  21st May, 1946.

xi

I

OUR VILLAGE

KYLE OF LOCHALSH is built round its railway and harbour, and these are the main supports of its population. When I first came to live there, it consisted of a miscellaneous collection of about eighty dwellings. Several were comfortable stone-walled buildings, but others were constructed of wood and corrugated iron.

The village presented a new, out-west appearance. Houses had been erected on rocky hillside, in hollow or crevasse ; in short, wherever the ingenuity of man or the avarice of landowner permitted.

The inhabitants numbered about three hundred and fifty. Some had migrated from neighbouring townships. Many came from more distant parts of the country. There were English, Irish, and Welsh whom we classify as Sassenachs. There were lowland Scots from Aberdeen, Fife, and Glasgow, and these were also regarded as aliens—unless they spoke " the Gaelic".

What a difference that makes ! Speak the old tongue, and though you come from the ends of the earth—Gaelic is still spoken in Canada and New Zealand—you will be welcomed as a true Celt.

The railway cuts through the centre of the village and terminates at a square-built pier at which steamboats call. This in turn is intersected by the highway from the east which ends at the Skye ferry pier.

From a window in my modest pharmacy I looked in

those early days across the ferry to the Isle of Skye. I feasted my eyes upon the beauty of Beinn-na-Caillich, with its mantle of mist ; I saw the ships as they passed daily to and from Portree and Stornoway.

In Summer the bay was dotted with small boats. Captain Finlayson, owner of the first motor-boat in the district, was crossing and re-crossing with passengers. Many a tale could the Captain tell of his exploits in the Yellow Sea in the days when he sailed his ship to China and the Far East.

Peter Leitch and his stalwart crew rowed the old garboard, a heavy flat-bottomed boat built for ferrying sheep and cattle. Across it were two planks upon which a motor car had to be precariously perched.

It was dry work rowing this heavy boat, and the sum of one pound divided among six men was little enough recompense for their labours.

A disgruntled medico from the east thought differently.

" The charge is preposterous," he raved. " I shall report you to the railway company. What is your name ? "

" Leitch," was the reply.

" A damned funny name," was the sour comment.

Mr. Leitch related this incident to me. He did not object to the doctor questioning his charge, but he did resent any disparaging allusion to his name.

" What's funny about my name ? " he asked me plaintively ; then, presumably having in mind the term applied to members of the noble profession, added, " After all, he is a leech himself."

From another window I saw up the village street, one side lined with bank, post-office, and shops, the other with bank, hotel, and gardens. In the distance a heather-clad hill loomed up.

The street showed signs of utter neglect. It was hollowed out with the traffic of years ; and on wet days—which occurred with a persistence worthy of a better cause—a muddy stream followed a zig-zag course down the centre.

This rendered it difficult for any but the well-shod pedestrian to cross, a fact only appreciated by the village shoemaker, a kindly man with a large wife and numerous family to support.

One side of the roadway was regarded as a dumping place. There were heaps of stones, empty boxes, and barrels. Alongside shopkeepers' barrows an ancient four-wheeler, inscribed " Loch Duich Royal Mail," added to the general untidiness.

This vehicle, usually referred to as " The Mail," came to rest there daily in the middle of the forenoon. It remained until the arrival of the " morning " train from the South—actually in the late afternoon.

After the mails were sorted—perhaps sometimes unofficially censored—leisurely preparations were made to depart. Horses were yoked, packages were collected from nearby shops, and perhaps a final call made farther up the street.

Bags of mails were brought from the Post Office and carefully stowed away, with probably a venturesome passenger perched uneasily on top. Then Sandy Campbell climbed on board, picked up the reins, and with a " tally-ho " in Gaelic, set out with his load for Balmacara and Aird Ferry.

The road meanders round corners and up steep hill-sides. Passengers had to get out to walk up the steep places and sometimes even to walk down the other side. As there is practically no level road, travelling by 'bus was little more than a courtesy description. But the four-shilling fare was a concrete fact.

Sandy Campbell was a popular worthy, but in spite of his popularity his horses always brought him safely home. When one of these died he invested in a motor-bus. It was a poor substitute for horses. These had been his old friends. Besides they had often fed by the wayside, but his engine required supplies of fuel. This cost money.

So it was rumoured that Sandy had increased the fare. One day I happened to meet the Reverend Mr. Fraser, minister of Glenshiel, as he stepped off the 'bus. I asked him what was now the fare.

" Well," said Mr. Fraser, " I have heard that Sandy has increased it to five shillings ; but I just hand him four shillings as usual. Sandy looks at me, but," he added pawkily, after a pause, " I'll not be seeing him ! "

The Post Office was part of a somewhat pretentious building which also housed the offices of the Bank of Scotland. The postmaster, Mr. Ewen Macdonald, was youthful and energetic. His staff consisted of a bevy of bright young women, some with dark hair and others blessed with auburn, copper-coloured or flaming red locks.

Who would not have been a postmaster ? Is it any wonder that the Post Office was known locally as " The Harem " ?

Mr. Macdonald told me that canvassing for an appointment was strictly forbidden. Then he added inconsequently, " I used to play shinty with Ian Macpherson (our local Member of Parliament) at Kingussie ! "

A large number of sub-offices under the charge of the Kyle postmaster had to be inspected periodically. Such

KYLE OF LOCHALSH AND KYLEAKIN

journeys had to be made in all states of the weather ; and roads being bad and conveyances primitive, the traveller required to be warmly clad. Mr. Macdonald related the following experience.

He had spilt some grease on his trousers. He was blessed with a careful young wife, who had sought to remove the stain with petrol. Unfortunately things are not always what they seem, and the petrol tin had contained paraffin.

However, its application apparently removed the stain; in fact, so pleased was Mrs. Macdonald with the result, that she applied paraffin liberally to the remainder of the garment, leaving it in her opinion " like new."

For a time Mr. Macdonald shunned the aromatic garment like the plague ; but, before he set out one wet day for the wilds of Kintail, his wife persuaded him that the fresh air of the mountains would put matters right.

It is a long journey to Kintail, and on the way back Mr. Macdonald called at the Aird Ferry Hotel for tea. Seated in the hotel verandah with Mr. Cameron, the proprietor, they were enjoying a quiet smoke when suddenly Mr. Cameron sniffed, then jumped to his feet.

" Confound those girls," he cried, " I can smell the paraffin. They have turned up the lamps too high again and the whole place will be smoked black."

He tramped off to reprimand the girls, but he need not have worried. It was only the postmaster's trousers !

Sandy Post was one of the most popular officials at the Post Office. Mr. Alexander Macrae, to give him his full appellation, had a sandy red beard which lent to him a false impression of age. He was so hard worked that sometimes he had barely time to read the post cards.

Youthful members of the community had been known to play tricks on him.

One afternoon, as Sandy was delivering letters at the pier, he became the possessor—how, I have not enquired—of a " fry " of herrings. He placed them carefully under an empty fish-box, to remain there until he had completed his delivery.

Someone, noting Sandy's action, quietly removed the fish, hiding them elsewhere. Screened from observation, this practical joker watched Sandy's return. He arrived, lifted the box, and bent down to remove his fry.

For a moment he gazed in utter disbelief. Then he straightened himself ; he found voice. Fascinated bystanders listened breathlessly as he poured out a torrent of invective. First in English, then in more expressive Gaelic, he denounced " the pack of thieves from whom no honest man's goods were safe." He went into lurid details about their ancestry, ending up by depicting the climatic conditions of their future abode.

One thing which struck me very forcibly at first was the happy-go-lucky, care-free manner in which business was conducted. When a consignment of goods arrived by rail or steam-boat they were allowed to remain in a goods' shed at the station until called for.

Local merchants sometimes wheeled up their own merchandise, incidentally borrowing a railway barrow for the purpose. Others who were prepared to wait the convenience of the local carter, Mr. William Johnstone, might avail themselves of his services.

If not otherwise engaged, Mr. Johnstone would arrive from the nearby village of Erbusaig, along with horse and cart, in the middle of the forenoon. He was a handsome, finely-built man, with long flowing white beard. He made a striking figure as, with his black horse yoked to high-wheeled cart, he went about delivering goods from railway or pier.

In his younger days he had gone to sea ; and for some time he had served on a yacht of the Kaiser, with whom he was a favourite. Now he was content to be the village carter. Ach, the German whisky was not goot !

The Kyle Hotel, which occupies a commanding position at the top of the main street, is an enlarged edition of the old Kyle Inn which existed long before there was a railway in the West. Mr. Urquhart was its genial host. An ardent Free Churchman, he provided free accommodation for ministers of his denomination. This generous gesture sometimes led to unforeseen results.

On one occasion the Reverend John Mackay, Minister of Plockton, after partaking of a substantial meal there, including liquid refreshments, called for his bill.

" One shilling," he was told.

" Nonsense," he said, " There must be some mistake."

He explained what he had got ; but the maid was emphatic.

" Just a shilling," she insisted.

Mr. Mackay paid cheerfully, at the same time remarking that this was the cheapest hotel he had ever visited.

" Perhaps they think you are a ' Wee Free,' " suggested a fellow guest.

Now Mr. Mackay was a minister of the " Established " Church. He was evidently receiving a concession meant only for the ministers of the " Wee Free " Church—a rival denomination. He was despoiling the Egyptians !

It was a situation after his own heart.

2

EARLY DAYS

THE main street of the village stretched north, humble cottages lining the route wherever it was possible to build. Above and beyond those dwellings there rose the heather-clad hills on which an occasional sheep sought hopefully for a bite. These hills were no use for pasture ; it was impracticable to cultivate them. One wondered why they had not been built upon.

It was only twenty years since the railway had been extended to Kyle. With the exception of two hotels and one or two dwelling-houses, all buildings had been erected within that period. Here surely had been a splendid opportunity to build a well-planned town.

The estate at this time was owned by Sir Kenneth Matheson, Baronet of Lochalsh, one of Scotland's many absentee landlords. He was a son of the late Sir Alexander Matheson, Bart., M.P.

The story of Alexander Matheson is one to warm the heart of every Highlander. This wonderful man emigrated in his youth to India, returning home a millionaire fourteen years later. He bought Lochalsh and vast tracts of land in Ross-shire and Inverness. He built Inverinate House and Duncraig Castle. He became Member of Parliament and was created a baronet.

Surely an enthralling story—a story to inspire the son who succeeded to the estate. And here, when the railway was extended to Kyle of Lochalsh, was opportunity knocking at the door. Here was virgin land waiting to be built upon. Here was a chance to plan a town that not even the beautiful city of Bath could have surpassed in beauty.

Picture such a town. See the rocky hillsides picturesquely dotted with modern homes rising in pine-clad terraces to the hill-tops. Picture these dwellings facing the sunny south and the glorious west, sheltered from cold blasts and within sight of some of the most wonderful scenery in creation.

And picture our village to-day.

I have mentioned only the uninspiring dwellings in our midst, comfortable in a lukewarm way but not such as to arouse enthusiasm. But there was one delightful place, hidden away behind the village and approachable only by a narrow track winding past back-doors and cow-sheds. This road led to the Plock of Kyle, an irregularly shaped peninsula about a square mile in area.

The name of the Plock is derived from the Gaelic *An Ploc*, meaning " a lump." The cart track which began so obscurely meandered across the hillside and led down to a fertile plain about a mile from the village. Here there had been two crofts. These were now uncultivated and the old homesteads falling to ruins.

I often walked to the Plock in the early morning before business hours. Here I could sit on the heather, feasting my eyes on islet and loch and distant mountain, watching the morning clouds rise above the Cuillins, flit across the sky, and vanish. Like Ruskin I could say :

" Clouds and mountains have been left to me."

Again I felt that our laird had no vision. For here, on the high ground, was an ideal situation for building hotels and private residences ; and the pasture land below was capable of providing a sporting golf course.

At the extreme end of the peninsula lay a fine sandy beach, with two islets nearby, these only requiring connecting walls to form an enclosed bathing pool. But the utter unsuitability of the only approach from the village rendered any possibility of improvement or development very improbable.

A walk round the railway pier proved a never-ending source of interest. Boats from Stornoway and the Isle of Skye called each morning with passengers for the south, and again in the afternoon on their way north. In the mornings there were often fishing-boats laden with their catches of the previous night.

Even on Sundays during the fishing season there was liveliness about the harbour and station, special trains being run with the perishable cargo. For the wave of Sabbatarianism, which was to break out and spread over the Highlands a few years later, was yet undreamt of. In fact, when the Sunday loading and despatching of fish did actually cease, this was brought about mainly by the workers who wanted extra pay. Fish-buyers had not yet developed their extreme Sabbatarian views.

The village of Kyleakin, looking so bright and clean and nestling so picturesquely at the foot of Beinn-na-Caillich, early tempted me to cross to Skye. Captain Finlayson's motor-boat was waiting as I reached the ferry pier, and we quickly skimmed over the smooth sea.

The ferry-boat at that time touched a black wooden pier, up which the passengers had to climb. This pier had been built in order that the Portree boat—the old *Glencoe*—could call in at Kyleakin on its way to and from Kyle. In practice it was found that this was impossible at low tide, and the unsightly outgrowth has now been removed.

The main part of Kyleakin stands on a sandbank, although another portion, apparently older, which is reached by crossing the Obbe, has been built on the rocky base of the sheltering hills. The Obbe is an inlet of the sea, which at high tide flows inland, almost surrounding the newer part of the village.

Viewed from any direction, Kyleakin presents a delightful picture. Seen from the north, the ruins of Castle Moyle stand out grandly against the hills of Ardintoul, with the Five Sisters of Kintail towering in the distance.

As I set out to walk to the old castle I wondered that the community had not been enterprising enough to construct a decent path. After all, the village was not only a fishing port ; the people were partly dependent on Summer visitors for a livelihood.

But no, it is the same cry all over the Highlands— " Let the Government do it." One is sometimes tempted to believe that there may be a grain of truth in the old story of the Islander who lay on his back and sang :

> " Oh that the peats would cut themselves,
> The fish jump on the shore,
> And that I and my plaidie
> Could lie for aye and evermore.
> Oich ! Oich ! "

To reach the castle the Obbe had to be crossed. The tide was low and I managed to scramble across the muddy streamlet. Hidden away somewhere there was an ancient wooden bridge, and since then there has been erected a more substantial one.

I made my way past houses which had looked so delightfully picturesque at a distance, but which could be so exasperatingly placed when one wanted to pass. Here rapid progress was not encouraged. I walked in front of one dwelling, behind another, along what appeared to be the right path, only to find myself at a cow-shed.

After exploring various cul-de-sacs I reached the hill track beyond the village, but even then progress was hampered ; for there was not only one path, there were several. These had been made by sheep, goats, and cattle. They led in all directions. Eventually I reached the shore below the castle and quickly scrambled up the rocky height.

Only part of the ruined keep remained standing. With walls eleven feet thick, Castle Moyle must have been considered an impregnable fortress in its day. It is said to have been built by a Mackinnon of Strath who had married a Norse king's daughter known as " Saucy Mary." According to legend, Mary caused a chain to be stretched across the channel to the mainland, thus preventing ships passing until they had paid toll.

Although Plockton, six miles east of Kyle, is the nearest mainland village of any importance, there are other interesting hamlets and townships. Badicaul is only a mile distant, and although recently many of the houses have been—perhaps unfortunately from an aesthetic point of view—improved and modernised, they looked very attractive in those early days.

One beautiful cottage was owned by Mrs. Mackenzie, a charming old lady as delightful as her home. A well-thatched roof was supported by whitewashed stone walls, with small sunken windows and a low doorway at which one had to stoop to enter.

I called to see Mrs. Mackenzie one afternoon and she gave me a warm welcome. When I told her that my mother was a Mackenzie she was delighted. It was a bond. Oh, ye Lowlanders, ye Shakespeareans, what's in a name? Ye cannot understand.

The interior of the kitchen was spotless. On a crook above the cheery peat fire burning on the low stone hearth, there hung a black iron kettle. The lid rattled. It was a signal that the water was boiling—the modern enamelled article gives no such indication—and Mrs. Mackenzie was waiting, teapot in hand. Soon we were enjoying a cup of tea with oatcakes and home-made jam. Nectar!

Beyond Badicaul the road dips down to Erbusaig. Whitewashed cottages spread picturesquely round the bay, the waters of which at high tide almost lapped the doorsteps. The view was less pleasant at low tide when the waters receded beyond a high railway embankment, leaving a rough uninviting foreground.

I walked out to Erbusaig one early morning, and on this occasion I had a companion with me. I had hoped to get a photograph of a spinning wheel, with my companion spinning, but when we reached the village there was no sign of life. In those days at anyrate the people were of a good conscience and slept soundly.

At length a door opened and a tall man walked out into the morning sunshine. It was my friend Johnstone. No, he could not lend a spinning wheel. The people in the village did not now wear home-spun garments. It was cheaper to buy the mass-manufactured product.

About this time I conceived the idea of a series of photographs depicting Highland life. My difficulty was the human element. On one occasion I came upon an idyllic scene. A young mother and her two children were seated on a grassy mound. In the background was a trim thatched dwelling with nearby peat-stack.

C

I asked permission to photograph them, and the mother agreed. Before I could check her she went indoors with the children and did not reappear for some time. Then what a transformation! It was painful. They were ready for church but not for my camera.

A girl cousin on holiday offered to take the part of a milk-maid. The title of the picture was to be in Gaelic. We must make a success of it. With some trouble we got the cow, we got the stool, we got the pail. My cousin sat down. No, the cow did not kick, she was one of the quiet kine.

I considered the photograph a success, but I had not reckoned with the bucolic experts. These told me it was all wrong, for my cousin sat facing the tail instead of the head. It seemed to me immaterial how she sat, so long as she got the milk.

I had not realised that even a good Presbyterian can be very ritualistic when it comes to milking a cow!

3

THE BURGH OF BARONY

ALTHOUGH there is a railway station at Plockton this fact did not prove particularly helpful when I wanted to visit it in the early morning. True, a train ran each week-day at six o'clock, but there was no return one until a variable hour in the afternoon. Not relishing the idea of a six miles' walk back, I resolved to go by cycle in spite of the bad road. As it turned out, I had to walk much of the way in each direction owing to the hilly roads and poor surface.

There was no sign of life as I wheeled past Erbusaig. No peat reek ascended from the chimney of Mr. Johnstone's dwelling ; he was probably still in bed, reliving in dreamland the hectic days of his youth. The road is fairly level until the bridge across the Erbusaig Burn is reached. Here the Plockton road branches off.

I made no attempt to pedal up the steep hill road ; the walk was sufficient to leave me breathless when I reached the summit. It was a perfect morning. In front, across the moor, lay the Lily Loch in a hollow of the hills ; and away beyond, across the waters of Loch Carron, the peaks of high hills showed up above the morning mists.

There was a gradual descent all the way to Drumbuie. Keeping careful grip of my handlebars I bumped leisurely down the winding road, passing the spot where my friend Mr. Donald Matheson had suffered mishap. Incidentally, Mr. Matheson is known universally by another name, to which he refuses to answer—he asks to be addressed by the name which he uses when signing cheques.

On the night of his misfortune he had been detained at Kyle on important business which had terminated abruptly when the magic words, " Time, gentlemen," had been uttered. He hurriedly mounted his bicycle and made for home.

Speeding down this hill, a gust of wind caught his hat and whirled it aloft. Now the hat was a good one, and its owner instinctively raised both hands in an attempt to rescue it. But he was not quick enough. The hat sailed away over the moors ; and the bicycle, bereft of a guiding hand, forsook the narrow way.

So it happened that Mr. Matheson rested for a time,

and there are worse places than a ditch for quiet reflection. After all, experience adds to knowledge, and my unfortunate friend may have recalled the words of Cowper,

> " Experience, slow preceptress, teaching oft
> The way to glory by miscarriage foul."

Yet I fancy he was not much concerned about the way to glory.   On the contrary, Mr. Matheson was bound for Plockton !

Faint wisps of smoke were beginning to rise from the chimneys as I approached Drumbuie.   The peat fires, banked up on the previous night, had been stirred to life. Mr. Alexander Mackenzie, accompanied by his collie dog, was having a look round, and I noticed Mrs. Matheson early astir, but apart from these there was no sign of activity.

At Duirinish, half a mile farther on, one woman was already at work in the fields.   She was Mrs. Anstruther Mackay—there could be no mistaking that striking figure. She was dressed in heavy woollen jersey, short skirt of some strong unattractive material, and thick hob-nailed boots.

Those who have read the prophecies of the Brahan Seer may recall that the last of the Seaforths was doomed to marry a crofter.   It so happened that Mrs. Mackay was the last of the female line.   Obviously she had to marry a crofter ;   there could be no shirking of fate.

Anyhow Mrs. Mackay was a determined, staightforward type ;   she attempted no silly subterfuge such as marrying a gentleman farmer.   No, she married a plain, simple son of the soil.   She did more ;   she took him to London and introduced him to society.

Those were the days before such things were done. Even to-day such an action would meet with the disapproval of many in the Highlands. Indeed there are old families who still keep aloof from the wealthy lords of plebeian stock. They put caste before cash, too often ignoring the fact that caste is merely pride of descent from some successful cattle thief.

Mrs. Mackay's married life was a brief one. Her husband early succumbed to the strain, after which she carried on the croft, doing practically all the work on it single-handed. She was in everything thorough.

At this time the Duchess of Buckingham and Chandos occupied Duncraig Castle, and Mrs. Mackay was always a welcome guest there. It was noticeable that while Mrs. Mackay might be a typical crofter's widow by day, with the approach of eventide the sordid garments were discarded. Then, gowned and jewelled, she would step into the carriage sent from the castle, and drive off to dine with the Duchess. But the Brahan Seer did not foretell this !

Duirinish is pleasantly situated near the banks of the river. Beyond it is a high ivy-covered bridge from which a splendid view of the village is obtained, with the stream in the foreground and the Skye mountains looming up in the distance.

A short distance beyond the bridge the road branches off to Duncraig Castle and Strome Ferry. I continued along the Plockton road, down the steep Strathie Brae and on past the station. The substantial road bridge across the railway had evidently been built to span a double track of rails. But only a single track had been laid. The dream of some optimist had not come true.

It was high tide as I pedalled down the narrow road which leads to Plockton. I met the village carter, Mr. MacKellar, already intent on business. He and his faithful donkey were on their way to the station, to return no doubt heavily laden with supplies for the village shops, or it might even be with a barrel or jar for the hotel.

On the hillside above the roadway, part of a field has been enclosed by a fence and high stone wall. This forms the sanctuary where the Free Church has held its out-door Communion services for generations past. The congregation enters by a door in the high wall which serves the dual purpose of giving seclusion and providing protection from cold winds.

Within the enclosure is a grass-covered hollow, three sides created by Nature, probably with some degree of human assistance so that the seating might be as comfort-able as possible.

The view, on approaching the village, was incompar-ably beautiful. Along the shore stretched the winding street, lined with houses wedged closely together, all commanding a fine view of the sheltered bay now dotted with fishing-craft and pleasure boats.

In the foreground stood the Higher Grade School, its interesting spire reflected in the dark waters of an inlet into which the sea penetrates only at high tide. To the right rose the high cliffs of Craig, the Castle of Duncraig standing up grandly among the pine-clad crags. Away in the distance, across the waters of Loch Carron, towered grey peaks and mountain ridges.

Above the school doorway the Matheson coat-of-arms has been carved, the school having been built by the late Sir Alexander Matheson. Adjoining the school is the Parish Church with the churchyard in front, neither of which looked inviting that morning as I passed by.

The main street, which had seemed so perfect in the distance, did not attract when viewed at close quarters.

PLOCKTON

Some of the houses looked past their first youth ; indeed, as I was to learn later, many of the inhabitants were in the same position. But there need be nothing unlovely about age, and certainly most of the older houses looked clean and picturesque.

At one time Plockton was a ship-building centre of note, it being then the principal seat of industry in the parish. The school, still the best on the Western mainland, has been famed for generations, many doctors, sea captains, and others in various walks in life having received their early education there.

As far back as 1808, the town was erected into a Burgh of Barony in favour of Hugh Innes of Lochalsh, Esquire.

Recently I asked Sheriff Trotter, an Edinburgh K.C., to explain the meaning of a burgh of barony. My friend's face shone, he straightened his shoulders and spoke. He spoke fluently, eloquently, convincingly for half an hour ; but when he had ended I knew no more.

There are others, it would appear, who are still in the same state of happy ignorance. I have in mind a large town in a northern county which recently proposed to confer the freedom of the burgh on a distinguished—and wealthy—townsman.

A hitch arose when it was discovered that a Royal charter of some antiquity could not be traced. The town was a police burgh, but such towns do not confer " freedoms." Then it was remembered that it had also a charter as a burgh of barony. The situation was saved ; and in due course the freedom ceremony took place, to the accompaniment of the usual speeches interspersed with the usual quenching of persistent thirst.

So far, Plockton has not conferred the freedom of the

burgh on anyone. No, the people of this delightful
village, so marvellously blessed in its surroundings,
planted in such an ideal setting for the tourist, have not
yet wakened to the value of advertisement.

One day they may bestir themselves. Once let them
realise the possibilities, they will honour their distinguished
townsmen and wealthy benefactors. They will reward
them with burgess tickets, which, to ensure full Press
publicity, will no doubt be inscribed in Gaelic.

Till then, Plockton, Burgh of Barony, sleep on.

4

A CRUISE UP LOCH DUICH

IT is difficult to understand why Highlanders, a proud
race ever ready to fight, suffered so tamely during the
Highland Clearances which occurred nearly a hundred
years ago. The usual procedure was for the landowner or
chief to spend most of his time—and what money he could
extort from his tenants—carousing in London or Paris.

In these haunts, where he was in all probability
looked upon as a simple barbarian, he was readily fleeced.
So the cry for more money came back to the Highlands.
The miserable hirelings who were left in charge of the
estates drained the people of every penny they possessed
and then proceeded to evict them. The land could be put
to more profitable use.

Naturally the Government did not bother about the
plight of men they did not require, for the wars were over for
the time being, and there was no immediate need for soldiers.

They had never heard of the old Gaelic saying, "Where there are no boys in arms, there will be no armed men."

So the evictions and atrocities went on ; then, when the glens were deserted, the Government woke up. Its leaders were roused to action. They appointed a Royal Commission !

Of all the stories of the Clearances, that which gives me greatest satisfaction to recall is one about Kintail. It is a tale of poetic justice such as one rarely experiences in real life.

Seaforth evicted a large number of tenants from the lands of Kintail. His factor, Duncan Mor MacRae, carried out the evictions—and added much of the land to his own extensive sheep farm. Men of his own clan were rendered homeless ; they were driven into exile to satisfy the greed of their callous kinsman and their selfish chief.

Men and women, young children and the aged, all were driven from their homes. Perhaps the most bitter pang of all was the realisation that their chief, for whom they would have given their lives, had no further use for them. All he wanted was money, and they had none to give.

Taking with them their scanty possessions, they crossed the Atlantic in a filthy boat, herded like cattle. After enduring great hardship they finally settled at Glengarry in Canada. In that hospitable land they prospered, and their descendants live there to-day, a thriving community.

But what of the factor and his chief ?

" The laird is bad enough," says an old proverb, " But the factor is the devil himself."

Alas for Duncan Mor MacRae's schemes ! He died ruined and penniless. As for Seaforth, he was obliged to sell his inheritance.   And the last of his race has passed on.

It was to view this former land of Seaforth that I set out by motor-boat, along with three companions, Stewart, Ross, and Fraser.   On a clear frosty morning in late September our boat skimmed rapidly over the calm waters of Loch Alsh.

On our left stood out the Murchison Monument, a grey granite obelisk, erected in memory of Colonel Murchison who had collected the rents and defended the lands of his outlawed chief.   A faithful steward.   An honest factor.   No wonder there is a monument to his memory !

On our right lay Ardintoul, a green oasis sheltered by the mountain ridge which separates it from Glenelg.   As we approached the mouth of Loch Duich we saw on our left the ruins of Eilean Donan Castle, the full story of which I was to learn later.

Beyond the Castle was the village of Dornie, its trim dwellings built along the side of the narrow street which stretches up the side of Loch Long.   The spire of St. Duthac's Church, standing by the ruined monastery, was just visible in the distance.   The ferry-boat was crossing and re-crossing between Dornie and Aird Ferry.

We passed Totaig on our right, with nearby the ruins of Castle Grugach, a large circular dun.   The tide was in our favour as we sped quickly up Loch Duich.   Ahead rose grandly the Five Sisters of Kintail, their peaks tipped with the first of the coming winter's snows, and their whole outline clearly reflected in the placid waters of the loch.

We landed at the Royal Pier, Letterfearn.   This jetty was built for the convenience of the late King Edward VII when his yacht visited the famous loch.   Surely no more enchanting scene had ever met the eyes of this hardened admirer of beauty. He thought the Five Sisters the most wonderful he had seen. In his day he had known many sisters. He could speak from experience!

The picturesque village of Letterfearn, not yet spoilt by too many modern improvements, stretched away in straggling fashion along the lochside. A narrow but level road led to the head of the loch. We passed Ratagan, a modest mansion where James Hogg, the Ettrick Shepherd, had stayed. Above us towered Mam Ratachan, up whose steep sides the road from Shiel to Glenelg winds.

I noticed an empty dwelling, rather out of keeping with its surroundings. It was a well-built two-storey building with large oriel windows. It was uninhabited and had a forlorn look. Behind it was a charming cottage with low thatched roof.

Upon enquiry I found that both houses were attached to the same croft. A son had emigrated, and in due course had sent home the money to build a modern house for the comfort of his parents.

They had allowed him to do so, knowing that it would give him pleasure; but when the time came to leave the warmth of the old home for the colder comfort of the new— they simply could not do it. So the white house became a white elephant.

From this point there is an extraordinarily fine view of these famed mountains, the Five Sisters of Kintail; with Ben Attow, readily distinguishable by its notched top, showing up behind. The picture provided by Nature does not please everyone, however.

I remember one occasion, some years after this visit, when an elderly gentleman of the explosive type was looking at what I regarded as a really good photograph. He glared at the picture. His face went purple.

" It is too well-balanced to be genuine," he told a
friend.   " It's a fake, a rotten fake.   No one ever saw the
Cuillins look like that."

He peered at the title, " The Five Sisters of Kintail".
I feared apoplexy ; but no, his sense of humour saved him.
He had discovered that the Cuillins were not the only
wonderful mountains in the West.

It was late afternoon when we left Letterfearn.   At
first the tide was against us and we made slow progress.
Then, near Avernish, we steered too far inshore.   A flat,
submerged rock barred our passage, and before we
realised our danger we were aground.

We attempted to push off with an oar, but in vain.
The tide was at its height and was beginning to recede.
Darkness was falling.   There was no help for it ; three
of us—Stewart, Ross, and I—stepped into the water and
commenced to push off.   We left Mr. Fraser on board,
for he had a wife and family.

At last, with a desperate heave, we got the boat off,
and away it went with the tide.   Mr. Fraser could not
start the engine, and his one oar was useless.

So there we stood, three men out of a boat, with the
cold sea swirling round our knees.   Land was in sight,
but we could not swim.

Fortunately we had been observed by those on shore.
A crofter pulled out in a small boat, and we were quickly
rescued and put on board our own vessel.

We got home without further incident, back to
warmth, comforting sleep, and dreams :

" Beneath thy spell, O radiant Summer sea,
     Lulled by thy voice, rocked on thy shining breast,
 Fanned by thy soft breath, by thy touch caressed,
     Let all thy treacheries forgotten be."

THE FIVE SISTERS OF KINTAIL, FROM LETTERFEARN

5

THE INVASION OF 1719

A N evening immersion in Loch Alsh in late September
is not to be recommended. After my experience I
found time to peruse the Publications of the Scottish
History Society in which is recorded Mr. Dixon's account
of the invasion of 1719.

Mr. Dixon's admirable account is too detailed for
inclusion here, so I shall relate as briefly as possible the
main incidents of that event. The whole episode savours
of Hollywood.

James Butler, an Irishman, second Duke of Ormonde,
planned, with the assistance of Spanish forces, to invade
Great Britain and set King James VIII. on the throne.

Like another monarch of a later age, James Stuart
was not particularly anxious to sit on a throne ; but that
did not prevent many, from various motives, from
supporting his cause. No doubt some of his friends were
more concerned about their own importance and advancement than about their king's rights.

The main expedition, consisting of five ships of war
with twenty-two transports carrying five thousand troops
with arms for thirty thousand men, set sail from Cadiz on
7th March, 1719. Three weeks later they encountered a
terrific storm lasting forty-eight hours. The flagship was
dismasted, the other ships crippled, and the whole fleet
scattered to the four winds. A second Spanish Armada
had failed.

Meanwhile, on 8th March, a smaller expedition had

set sail for Scotland, under command of the Earl Marischal.

On the 19th March, James Keith, brother of the Earl Marischal, left Havre in a ship of twenty-five tons ; and, sailing round the west coast of Ireland, arrived at Stornoway on 4th April. Here he found the Earl Marischal's frigates at anchor. On the following day Seaforth and Tullibardine arrived.

Chiefs and leaders now commenced wrangling for position. Tullibardine produced his commission as Lieutenant-General, whereupon the Earl Marischal resigned control, while still retaining command of the ships.

Although James Keith's ship had arrived at Stornoway on the 4th April, the actual date, according to British reckoning, was 24th March. Unlike Spain, which had adopted the Gregorian Calendar over a century previously, Great Britain was still using the out-of-date Julian Calendar.

Thirty more years were to elapse before the conservative British nation was to adopt the New Style ; and no doubt a considerably longer period before Stornoway fell into line. Douce Presbyterians, were they to be dictated to by a Pope ? Shame !

So it happened that, after spending eleven days in Stornoway, it was still the fourth of April when the expedition again put out to sea. They intended landing at Kintail, but owing to unfavourable winds did not reach Loch Alsh until the thirteenth, when they effected a landing.

Clan Ranald and Lochiel arrived a fortnight later, but there was still no word of the Duke of Ormonde. More conferences were held.

To-day we may regard these conferences as puny

affairs compared with those developed later by the League of Nations. Yet they served a similar purpose ; they gave the participants an opportunity to change their minds and save their faces.

Tullibardine wanted to re-embark and return to Spain, but the Earl Marischal had other views. He sent his two frigates back to Spain on 30th April, while his forces took up their quarters at Eilean Donan Castle.

A week later, five British ships, under the command of Captain Boyle, arrived on the coast. Three sailed through Kylerhea, and anchored at the mouth of Loch Alsh. The other two steered round the north of Skye, and anchored at Loch Kishorn.

Forty-five Spaniards guarded Eilean Donan Castle in which were most of the stores and ammunition. The main body of troops was encamped at Dornie.

On 10th May, Captain Boyle, with the three ships, *Worcester*, *Enterprise*, and *Flamborough*, sailed up the loch. The Captain sent an officer with a flag of truce to demand the surrender of the Castle ; but the Spaniards fired on the boat and did not allow it to land.

At eight o'clock that evening the British ships opened fire. A storming party landed, meeting with little resistance. The Spanish garrison was taken prisoner, provisions and ammunition captured, and the Castle blown up.

For two centuries Eilean Donan Castle was to remain a picturesque ruin, until restored by the late Colonel MacRae-Gilstrap. Opinions differ as to the propriety of restoring a ruin ; but it is generally admitted that the work of restoration has been carried out with wonderful perfection of detail.

The invaders were now cut off by sea ; they could not

even cross to Skye.   Besides, they were short of food and
ammunition.   Tullibardine resolved to raise a Highland
army ; but unfortunately the news of the dispersion of the
Cadiz fleet had now reached the Highlands.   Even the
thousand troops which he eventually raised were not very
enthusiastic.

On the 23rd May, Jacobites and Spaniards marched
to the head of Loch Duich.   A fortnight later, Lochiel
came with 150 men, Seaforth brought 500 more, and a son
of Rob Roy came with a few.

Meanwhile General Wightman set out from Inverness
with a force of 850 infantry, 120 dragoons, and 130
Highlanders.   News reached the Jacobites that he was
marching towards Kintail.

On the afternoon of 9th June, hasty preparations
were made for the reception of the Lowland forces.   A
position was selected near Shiel Bridge, about five miles
above Invershiel, and this was hurriedly fortified.   A
barricade was made across the road and along the face of
the hill.

Seaforth was on the extreme left, up the side of Scour
Ouran, with 200 of his best men.   Along with him were
the Earl Marischal and Brigadier Campbell.   The main
body consisted of the Spanish regiment, now reduced to
200, under its Colonel, Don Nicolas Borano ; Lochiel with
150 ; Sir John Mackenzie of Coul with 200 of Seaforth's
men ; and smaller numbers belonging to Mackinnon, Rob
Roy, Lidcott, and others.

Tullibardine commanded in the centre, accompanied
by Glendaruel.   The hill on the south bank, the right of
the position, was occupied by 150 men under Lord George
Murray.

The Hanoverian army marched to the attack on the

afternoon of 10th June. Between five and six in the
evening they advanced against Lord George Murray, on
the south of the river. The first attack was repulsed, but
after securing reinforcements they met with some success,
which, however, they were too slow-footed to follow up.

Several hours of hard fighting ensued ; but eventually
the Jacobites were driven back. The Hanoverian Army
pursued them over the shoulder of Scour Ouran, only
halting as darkness fell. Near the top of the mountain is
a corrie now known as the Spaniards' Pass.

Next morning the Spanish commander delivered his
sword to General Wightman, and, according to report,
everybody else " took the road he liked best."

After his doubtful victory, Wightman proceeded to
" terrify the rebels " by burning the homes of " the
guilty." The smug humbug ! Anyhow, the rebellion
was over.

During the battle an English officer, Captain Downes,
was killed. He was buried on the field of battle on the
south side of the river ; and, all Hanoverian soldiers being
classified as Dutch, his last resting-place is now known as
" The Dutch Colonel's Grave." Jacobite opponents,
bearing no malice, apparently conferred upon him the
posthumous promotion to the rank of colonel ! Not to be
outdone in courtesy, the Dutch colonel is said still to
frequent the glen on dark nights.

The participators in the rebellion now went their
ways. Seaforth made his peace with King George and
spent the remainder of his days at home. The Keiths
entered the service of Frederick the Great, the Earl
Marischal dying at Potsdam in 1788, " a man greatly
beloved."

Tullibardine raised the Prince's standard at Glen-

D

finnan in 1745, and died the following year in the Tower
of London.

6

A DAY AT GLENELG

THE old *Glencoe* sailed daily between Portree and
Mallaig, calling at Raasay, Broadford, and Kyle of
Lochalsh ; also, on certain days, at Glenelg and Armadale.

I chose a good morning to visit Glenelg. The veteran
paddle-boat came churning alongside the Kyle pier and
was tied up. Although its arrival was a daily occurrence,
the event never failed to rouse fresh wonder, fresh excitement.

East-bound passengers from Skye disembarked ;
sundry hampers, boxes, and bales were loaded on to the
ship and stored away, more or less carefully ; then a flock
of sheep was driven up the narrow gangway. At last the
passengers were permitted to go on board.

Away we sailed down Loch Alsh, Captain Baxter
standing erect on the bridge. There are many stories told
about the worthy Captain. His religious beliefs were
particularly clean-cut. What he believed, he believed.
He had no use for expediency or compromise ; he would
have failed miserably as an archbishop.

On one occasion, I have been told, a member of " the
cloth" fell over the side of the ship. The cry was raised,
" Minister overboard."

" What denomination ? " demanded the Captain.

" Wee Free," was the reply.

The command came swiftly, " Full speed ahead."

I had not had much experience of sea travel, beyond an occasional trip between Aberdeen and the Orkneys. Even the quaint slogan, " Passengers keep abaft the binnacle," looked exciting, until the binnacle turned out to be merely the compass-box. Still, it was nice to be " abaft."

The greater part of the deck upon which I, along with a few other passengers, stood, had a wooden barricade stretched across. Behind this, a flock of sheep was herded. I concluded, prematurely optimistic, that we were all travelling at the freight rate for sheep.

Lachie, the purser, was to disillusion me. He came to collect the fares, and I handed over the sum asked for. Then I glanced at my ticket. The sheep, it appeared, were travelling first-class !

Although Lachie has now gone to his fathers, he is still a well-remembered figure. He was very faithful in the service of David MacBrayne, but it may be that there were some to whom this virtue did not commend him.

In the days of scarcity during the Great War, Lachie collected stray pieces of wool, sufficient to spin himself cloth for a suit. It was said that as he counted each sheep going on board, his hand unconsciously closed on a fresh tuft of wool !

The *Glencoe* churned her way round the Caillich, and through the Narrows of Kylerhea. On our left stood the old inn, a grey stone building, where Dr. Johnson and James Boswell had spent an uncomfortable night at the beginning of their memorable tour in Skye in 1773.

Beyond Kylerhea stretched the Sound of Sleat. To our left the bay opened out. Along its shores, bathed in the morning sunshine, lay the historic village of Glenelg.

Our ship cast anchor ; and nearby two men in a flat-bottomed rowing boat were waiting. A door in the side of the *Glencoe* was opened, and soon a considerable amount of cargo was transferred to the boat alongside.

I stepped into the quivering boat. There was nothing to hold on to, and it would not remain steady. After a scramble I found a seat between the bag of oatmeal and a bale of " soft goods."

The boatmen addressed me in English and carried on a conversation with each other in Gaelic. The irony of it ! I was visiting the birthplace of my father, the home of my kin, and I could not speak or understand a word of the old language.

It was high tide as we landed at the dilapidated stone pier. This, I learnt, would be high and dry at low tide. The main part of the original harbour had disappeared, and great banks of sand had been thrown up on the shore.

The inhabitants of Glenelg, I was told, wanted a new pier, one which large steam-boats could come alongside. The beautiful bay was to be spoilt by some hideous erection in order that the Glasgow boat might come alongside once a fortnight. There could, of course, be no traffic in this thinly-populated district to warrant such an expense.

At a time when small wayside railway stations are being closed because motor-omnibuses can provide a more frequent service, it would seem that, similarly, Glenelg might benefit by a more frequent motor-boat service.

Instead of this dream pier, the inhabitants should concentrate on getting a motor-launch to run two or three times daily between Kylerhea and Kyle of Lochalsh. At both these places there are already suitable piers. The only drawback to this plan is that a Government subsidy

would not be required.   And we do love to get Government grants !

A level road stretches round the coast to Eileanreach, where it crosses the Glenbeg river and winds up the hillside, continuing its tortuous course to Arnisdale on the shore of Loch Hourn.

I turned east at Eileanreach, and followed the farm road which leads up Glenbeg. What a glorious walk ! The roadside was bordered with rhododendrons, dog-roses, and wild flowers in profusion. An occasional rabbit hopped across the track, there was the murmur of the river below, and the chirping of birds overhead.

Across the river a waterfall, high up the mountain-side, gushed and sparkled as it came tumbling down over its rocky ledge.   The foaming waters plunged noisily to the hidden gorge below, emerging farther on to join the smiling river pursuing its peaceful course down the glen.

A short distance beyond, I came in sight of Dun Telve, one of several brochs in the vicinity.   It stands on the plain by the side of the river, high hills towering on either side.   According to tradition, the Picts built this dwelling with stones brought from a quarry high up the mountain on the other side of the glen.

Each stone was passed from hand to hand along a living chain of Picts. An early model of the Ford conveyer !

I continued my walk up the glen, reaching the farm of Corrary half a mile farther on.   I came upon my old friend, Angus Macleod, at that time tenant of Corrary farm, busily engaged removing the skin from a fine stag.

Angus immediately stopped his work to take me along to his house for a cup of tea.   A Highlander is always hospitable ; and in any case never requires much of an excuse to postpone a spot of work.   For once I was tactful enough not to enquire how he became possessor of the stag.

Dun Troddan, another Pictish dwelling, stands on the hillside above Corrary.   Both brochs are scheduled as ancient monuments and have been restored by the Government.   Miss M. E. Donaldson, in her *Wanderings in the Western Highlands and Islands* gives interesting details of them.

Returning to Glenelg, I walked along to the old church, an ugly building in lovely surroundings.   The road curves round the wall of the churchyard ;   then passes close to the Glenelg Hotel, a commodious building with an imposing frontage, beautifully situated.

The main street of the village presented a trim, clean, well-kept appearance.   It was probably little changed from the days when red-coats occupied the barracks, and the village belles were not too proud to be escorted by the Sassenachs.

East of the village, a narrow grass-covered road branches to the Barracks, now a ruin but still occupied at the time of Dr. Johnson's visit.   I followed the main route along a shady tree-lined avenue ;   then crossing a modern iron bridge which spans the Glenmore River, continued to the old smithy where the road forks.

Ahead stretched the winding road up the glen ;   to the left the road to Kylerhea ferry and the Isle of Skye branched off.   Along these roads, in pre-railway days, drovers from the Island came with their cattle as they set out on their long march to Falkirk.   At the time of my visit the ferry was closed and through traffic stopped, but now there is a good ferry service during the greater part of the year.

Outside the smithy sat the village blacksmith smoking

a pipe. It was a nice warm day, too warm for work. So Angus Stewart, alumnus of Aberdeen University, blacksmith of Glenelg, sat by his smithy door and meditated. The words of Jerome K. Jerome may have occurred to him :

" I like work ; it fascinates me. I can sit and look at it for hours, I love to keep it by me ; the idea of getting rid of it nearly breaks my heart."

Now Angus has gone to his rest ; the hot fires of his chequered youth are quenched. And the smithy fire no longer burns.

I resumed my leisurely ramble. Ahead stood the Manse, its back towards the mouth of the glen, so as to give a commanding view from as many windows as possible. All the doors were hidden away at the opposite side, sheltered by surrounding trees.

I met the Reverend Mr. Mactaggart, parish minister of Glenelg and a distinguished graduate of Edinburgh University. I was warmly welcomed by him and his charming wife.

It was near the hour of the mid-day meal, which I was invited to share. We were barely seated at the table when there was a knock at the door. A passing shepherd had called, and a place was at once made for him.

One or two extra at mealtimes was apparently nothing unusual. For the Manse is the House of the Open Door. Long may it remain so, and long may its beloved occupants remain to dispense hospitality and speed the traveller on his way.

Glenmore is a delightful glen to explore. The road ascends gradually, the river meanders below, and the great hills rise majestically. A peaceful, almost deserted glen, its once fertile acres now mostly uncultivated, it had at one time supported a hardy population.

Ninety years ago five hundred of the people of Glenelg, urged by a kind landowner to improve their lot, emigrated to Quebec. The old homesteads were burned, and the deserted holdings became one large sheep farm. There was no possibility of return.

As in the days of Jeremiah, the few who remained might have cried,

"Weep sore for him that goeth away ; for he shall return no more, nor see his native country."

On the hillside, opposite Scallasaig, stands a large stone which will one day fall down and kill a man ; for so the Brahan Seer has foretold. As so many of that worthy's prophecies have come true owing to the active co-operation of his admirers, one wonders who will rush forward to ensure the fulfilment of this one.

The Glenmore river is famed for its salmon. Scallasaig Lodge is picturesquely situated on its banks. As in many parts of the Highlands, the best dwellings are those reserved for sportsmen who occupy them for, at most, a few months in the year.

As I had arranged to return by the Glasgow steamboat *Claymore*, which was not due to call until the late evening, I spent the remainder of the day visiting relatives, most important of whom was my uncle. Oh, my prophetic soul, mine uncle !

My uncle was a gem. At that time he was about seventy years of age, well-built, over six feet in height, with a massive head of hair, bright twinkling eyes, and a humorous curve about the lips.

More than forty years previously he had selected the

best-looking young woman in the neighbouring parish of Kintail ; and together, regardless of parents, they had set out for Inverness, sixty miles distant, to get married. One was a Protestant and the other a Catholic, but such trifles did not worry them then nor at any time during their happy married life.

My uncle was a great walker. On one occasion he walked across the mountains to Lochaber, some sixty or seventy miles distant by the normal means of communication. He had no time to waste sitting in trains and steamboats. Besides, their routes were too circuitous. He believed in the direct method of approach.

He was noted for the speed and accuracy with which he could count sheep. As I began my day's outing herded with a flock of sheep on the *Glencoe*, I shall end up with a sheep-counting story, the accuracy of which I dare not vouch for, but which is certainly typical of my uncle's capacity for leg-pulling.

A visitor, watching him at work as a flock of sheep passed by, asked him how he managed to ascertain their numbers so quickly and correctly. He replied, with that twinkle which was seldom absent :

" Oh, it's quite simple. I just count their feet, and divide by four."

7

AN OUTDOOR COMMUNION

I HAD become the owner of a motor boat which, in honour of a distinguished visitor, His Highness the

Maharaja Gaekwar of Baroda, I had named the *Baroda*. It was a well-built craft, and, once it started—but that is another story—could outdistance any of its size in the locality.

It was Sunday morning, a glorious day in June. The engine had been recalcitrant and time had been lost, but now we were speeding across the glittering waves. Seated in the boat with me were two companions. Mr. Stewart, better known to his friends as Johnnie Stewart, was one day to be my " best man." And the other ? Well, why does one need a best man ?

We cut in between Kyleakin Lighthouse and the Mainland, a route not favoured by more experienced boatmen ; then away past Port-na-Cloich and on to Stromeferry. Here, before the railway was extended to Kyle, steamboats from the Isles made their daily calls. Now the wooden wharf stood gaunt and deserted.

The tide being in our favour, we made great speed up the smooth waters of Loch Carron. Ahead of us were boats of varying sizes and ages, motor, rowing, and sailing, all proceeding in the same direction. For this was the day of the Free Presbyterian Communion at Lochcarron, and the congregation was gathering from near and far.

This day was the culmination of a period of preparation. Thursday had been observed as a Fast Day, a Holy Day kept like a Sunday, a day on which no unnecessary work was done. Large congregations had attended the Fast Day services, also the special " Men's Day " service on Friday, the day of " Speaking to the question," called, in Gaelic, *Latha na Bodach*.

We landed on the shore at Slumbay, where large crowds were arriving. Some came on foot. Many young

AN OUTDOOR COMMUNION (From an old sketch)

people came by cycle. Old men and women came in carts and other vehicles of unbelievable age and diversity of appearance.

In many houses, visitors from a distance were spending the " Communion season " with their friends. They had arrived in time for Thursday's service, and would remain until Monday.

There was no church large enough to hold the multitude. The church, which normally held the whole congregation, was used on this day for services in English. The principal service, at which Holy Communion was to be celebrated, was conducted throughout in the Gaelic tongue ; and it was held in the open.

We approached " Young Donald's Wood," below which was the place set apart for the service. Collecting plates, placed on posts at convenient points, added a touch of reality to the scene. We sat down on the grass-covered slope of the hillside, the pine trees offering welcome shade from the scorching sun. In front of us stretched the blue waters of the loch, with the *Baroda* riding at anchor.

The principal minister was the Reverend Neil Cameron of Glasgow. Along with several other ministers he occupied a wooden tabernacle, not unlike a bathing box. This afforded the worthy divines a measure of protection from the sun or from an unexpected shower. The congregation had to be content with umbrellas.

The service began. The minister announced a metrical Psalm ; he read it over. The precentor stood up and " gave out the line." The congregation sat as they sang. The precentor intoned another line, the congregation repeated it, and so it went on to the end.

The minister prayed while the congregation stood. He prayed for the rich, the poor ; for black, for white ;

for the friend, the stranger, the exile ; for those on land, on sea, at home, or abroad. He prayed for those who went to church and those who stayed away. He prayed individually or collectively for every man, woman, and child on the face of creation.

But he did not pray for the dead. That would have been " Popery." I wonder was there any aching soul in that vast gathering who would have been comforted by a word spoken on behalf of some wayward one who was gone. Dear Christian brother, in letting the dead be damned, had you no pity for their living kin ?

More psalm-singing followed, more lengthy prayers— prayers of exhortation and prayers of denunciation. And what fervour !

Mr. Cameron spoke with peculiar knowledge of the feminine fashions of the day. He denounced the wearing of short skirts. " Down with them" was, in effect, his cry. One could not help wondering what would have happened if the reverend gentleman had penetrated to the Garden of Eden. It is hard to believe that Eve's frugal taste in lingerie would have met with his approval.

The solemn part of the service now commenced. The minister exhorted the faithful to go forward to the Communion Table. He warned them of the dangers of neglecting to do so. He told them that they were miserable worms, unworthy to live. He added that anyone who partook unworthily was damned for evermore. His hearers were confronted with a dilemma which might have baffled Solomon.

He read out another metrical Psalm, and announced that during its singing all intending communicants should take their places at the Communion Table. This Table consisted of a long wooden bench covered with a white linen cloth. On either side, planks supported on barrels had been placed to form seats.

The Song of David rose to the skies as a people, emotional, exalted, sang it with overflowing fervour. A few old men and women rose up and went slowly forward, sat down at the Holy Table, and bowed their heads reverently.

The Song ended. There was a pause. The minister further exhorted the congregation. The Psalm was sung again, to give them another opportunity to go forward ; a few more went. Another exhortation followed, another singing, another opportunity ; and so it went on. The irreverent thought which irresistibly arose was that the proceedings were now strangely like an auction sale.

Yet what a perfect picture ! Old men and old women, and one or two comparatively youthful ones of fifty or thereby, all clad in black, bent humbly before the Table. One sole patch of colour was added when Mr. Cameron sat down and covered his head with a Cameron tartan rug.

Presbyterians are often criticised because of the plainness, even the ugliness, of their churches. But here was a holy place set apart, its floor a carpet of living green, its canopy the blue sky, its walls the pine-clad rocks and the distant mountains. Was Roman temple ever half so grand ?

These men and women might be clad in sombre raiment, their hands gnarled with toil, but here were living saints. There were many who lived lives of self-sacrifice, working from dawn to dusk. They denied themselves all but the barest necessities of existence, in order that their children might receive a good education. They wanted them to have a better chance in the world

than their parents. Most Highlanders put education
before wealth.

Only a small part of the congregation partook of
Communion, while the others looked silently on. All
stood up as one of the ministers led in a prayer of thanksgiving, then sat down again to join in the singing of
another psalm.

The service dragged monotonously on. People began
to leave. They wandered off, two or three at a time, in as
inconspicuous a manner as possible, lest their going should
bring down on their heads the wrath of the ministers.

We too left the scene and visited a nearby house
where we enjoyed a cup of tea. We returned in time for
the benediction at 4.30 in the afternoon, the whole
service having lasted five hours.

The hungry worshippers quickly dispersed, some
going to their own homes and others to those of their
friends in the neighbourhood. In most of these houses tea
had been prepared, and in some cases a black bottle was
in evidence. For in the Highlands it may be truly said
that there is a great thirst after righteousness !

The minister is still all-powerful. He is loved and he
is feared. He is counsellor and friend in time of difficulty.
Doctors on the other hand, as a class, are not popular.
They are merely regarded as part of the evil of a sinful
world !

A minister who had recently retired from his parish,
related the following incident to me. He had been calling
upon members of his flock to bid them farewell. One old
lady was affected to tears.

" Good-bye, doctor, good-bye," she said ; then,
remembering he was the minister, added, " Eh, God
forgive me for calling you a doctor ! "

The stranger is sometimes puzzled by our religious denominations. In our village there were four brands of Presbyterianism. These were the Church of Scotland, known to its rivals as the " Established," the Free Church (" Wee Free "), Free Presbyterian (" Seceder "), and United Free Church. The last-mentioned has since united with the Church of Scotland, thus reducing the number of sects to three.

The system of church government is practically the same in all. They use the same Bible, the Authorised Version. They sing the metrical version of the Psalms ; and all, except the most extreme, sing hymns, although one sect confines itself to the singing of those hymns which are paraphrases of passages of Scripture.

To the onlooker, the particular type of hymn which each accepts or rejects constitutes the main sectarian difference. One is driven to the conclusion that religious fervour is sadly adulterated with " thrawnness "—a Scots word for which the English tongue can only provide such feeble equivalents as cussedness, perversity, or stubbornness.

There is a considerable element of spiritual pride in all these denominations. They are not oppressed by false humility. Each, like old Finlay Mackenzie, is firmly convinced that his brand of salvation alone is right.

Old Finlay dreamt that he had died and gone to Heaven. He was being shewn round the Celestial realm, with St. Peter as his guide.

" Who are these ? " he asked, seeing a great multitude.

" The Roman Catholics," was the reply.

Finlay was shocked. This was hard to believe.

" I did not think they would be here," he said. He shook his head sadly, then enquired, " And who are these away in the distance ? "

"Oh, these," answered St. Peter, "are the Established Church people. We let them wander where they like. They are well able to look after themselves."

So Peter then took Old Finlay by the hand and led him to a tent. A little band of old men, hoary, bald-headed, were seated at a bench, poring over the Book of Psalms. As they read they uttered occasional groans.

"Whisht," whispered St. Peter, "Don't make a noise. These are the Seceders, and they think there is no one here but themselves!"

8

THE KYLE COUNCIL

WE do not love originality. To be original is to be abnormal, a being to be shunned. To get a thing done, one must show that it has been done elsewhere. Our village is not unique in his respect. It is merely British.

Among us dwelt those who had been brought up in other surroundings. The ape-instinct is strong. They would make our village like their own. They would have street lamps. So a public meeting was called and a committee appointed.

Lamp posts were erected and oil lamps provided. The lamps were lit on dark nights and put out regularly at ten o'clock. The fact that the last steamer, ferry-boat, train, and 'bus left before dark, and that there was consequently little street traffic in the evening, was entirely disregarded. The feeble flicker of the oil-lamps proclaimed to an unseeing world that we were up-to-date.

The committee which looked after the lighting was one of many which had sprung up. Indeed, whenever there was a public grievance, real or imaginary, to be ventilated, it was the practice to call a public meeting. The speeches on such occasions varied according to circumstances, but the meeting inevitably terminated with the appointment of a committee.

The method of election to these bodies was simple. Donald stood up and nominated John who, in turn, proposed Donald. Then Angus got up and proposed Murdo ; and he, true to form, proposed Angus. So it went on until the number was complete or the whole audience elected.

Thus there existed a fantastic number of practically self-elected committees. Providentially these were usually inert, but if they did function, two or more would frequently overlap. It was felt that one public body, with sub-committees if necessary, might properly be elected to take over the duties of all.

Why not a town Council ? Kyle was not a burgh, not even a Burgh of Barony like its neighbouring village of Plockton. Nevertheless it might have a Village Council ; and, important point to remember, this would not be an innovation because several other villages, similarly situated, had appointed voluntary councils.

It was decided to call a public meeting to ascertain the feeling of the community. Full preparation was made before the date of meeting, a comprehensive scheme being worked out. The council was to consist of twelve members, with sub-committees for finance, amenities, lighting, and general purposes.

Mr. David Urquhart, M.A., headmaster of Kyle Public School, presided over the meeting. It was a large

E

gathering. There was much excitement and unusual unanimity. Nominations were made and polling-day fixed. It was also resolved to hold a heckling meeting on the eve of the poll.

Busy days followed. An electoral roll was compiled and posted up in a window of the village pharmacy. It gave the names of all persons of either sex, resident in Kyle, who had attained the aged of twenty-one years. This took place in May, 1919, and, sad to relate, was an innovation. It was to form a precedent for the extension of the parliamentary franchise nine years later !

Election addresses were now issued by candidates. These, either written or typed, were also posted up. Mr. Downie, fishery officer, wanted a road to the east. Mr. Fraser, laundryman, wanted a better water supply. Mr. Macdonald, railway guard, promised fresh milk.

One candidate wanted not only a tennis court but also a district nurse, presumably to partner him on the court. Another wanted the Parish Council to provide a telephone for the doctor. He planned getting married, and was looking ahead.

Mr. Hosack, banker, was absent at the Church Assembly in Edinburgh. He promised nothing ; and here the result of the poll was to point a moral.

Preparations were made for the heckling meeting. Little was left to chance. Mr. Downie, who had taken an active part in the scheme, sat up on the night before the meeting with a fellow-worker—I had almost said fellow-conspirator—preparing questions till the early hours of the morning.

The old Institute was packed when Mr. Urquhart presided over the first meeting of " electors." Heckling was slow at first ; but slips of paper, bearing questions in curiously similar caligraphy, soon appeared from various parts of the hall.

Many questions were personal. Mr. Anderson, postmaster, who had succeeded Mr. Macdonald, was asked if he thought it right to make one man do the work of a pair of horses. Sandy Post blushed unseen.

Mr. Mackintosh, railway guard, roused keen interest when he asked if the chairman of the Council would be called the Provost.

" Will he wear a chain of office ? " asked another. He had in mind the Provost of Kintore. A native of that Royal Burgh had been boasting to a stranger about the antiquity of his town.

" And we have a Provost," he concluded exultantly.

" Does he wear a chain of office ? " asked the visitor.

" A chain ? " was the reply, " Oh, no, we just let him go loose."

There was a record poll. The ballot-box was a biscuit tin with a slit in the lid. It was tied with red tape obtained from the post-office. Returning officer and clerk had been appointed and were in attendance. Even a representative of the law was there.

The counting of votes began. A crowd collected. Excitement was intense. Cheers greeted each result as announced. Twelve councillors, " good men and true," were elected.

A cart had been drawn up at the door of the Institute. The newly-elected members were helped into it—some were able to climb up unaided. A band of young men harnessed themselves to the shafts and set out at full speed down the village street.

Soon it became evident that their destination was the ferry. Most of the occupants, realising the position and being mainly non-swimmers, jumped out in time. Only Mr. Fraser, who suffered from a stiff leg, remained behind, and his captors spared him.

The work of the Council began. Mr. Hosack, who had made no promises, received most votes, and he was unanimously elected first Provost. Mr. John Maclennan, a prosperous fish-curer, who was next highest at the poll, was to be elected to the civic chair in the following year. For, in the democratic " constitution " of the Council, it was laid down that no-one could hold such high office for two consecutive years.

After various committees had been set up and filled, the Council, like most other public bodies, realised that the first matter requiring attention was finance. It was decided to hold a carnival, along with a jumble sale. A cart was sent through the village to collect unwanted articles. The response was overwhelming. All sorts of things—short of a stray husband—appeared to be unwanted.

The whole community turned out to the gathering which was held in the Drill Hall. There was something for everyone who came to buy, from a Harris Tweed suit to a grindstone. There was tea for the thirsty, and a fortune-teller for the credulous.

The Carnival provided entertainment for various temperaments. Provost Hosack and Bailie Murchison were in charge of the putting-green, laid with real turf inside the hall. Councillors Alexander Anderson and Murdo Macrae had a picture gallery of their own ; and the other councillors helped in some capacity.

The result was a complete success financially ; more, it had brought the various sections of the community together. Religious and political differences had not counted.   The inhabitants had worked together in perfect harmony for the common good.   A local newspaper, commenting on this fact, quoted the words of the Psalmist:

> " Behold how good a thing it is,
> And how becoming well,
> Together such as brethren are
> In unity to dwell ! "

The Council, being now provided with funds, immediately set to work.   At the instance of Mr. Anderson they decided to fix two annual public holidays.   Mr. Anderson disapproved of the number of Fast Days of various denominations, and thought the public holidays would supersede these.

He even imagined that his action would bring all the sects into line.   He was a newcomer and did not understand our mentality.   We were prepared to accept any number of workless days—but hands off the Fast Days ! So the net result was that the village got two additional holidays.

Street lighting received attention next.   The oil lamps which had smoked and flickered feebly were discarded, and in their place carbide lamps were provided. A meeting of the Council discussed the problem of more lamps.

" What's that ? " enquired Bailie Murchison who was somewhat deaf.

" They want a new lamp at the Established Church," explained the Provost.

Mr. Murchison, a staunch pillar of the Free Church, shook his head mournfully.

" More light for the Established Church ? " he said, " Indeed they are badly in need of it."

For a number of years there had been an outcry because there was no polling-station nearer than Plockton. The Council made representations on the matter, and were successful in having Kyle constituted a separate polling district, with polling station at the school.

The result was unexpected. Polling at Plockton, six miles distant, had meant for the Kyle electors a railway trip, a pleasant outing. It had meant meeting friends, and perhaps partaking of a cup of tea. It had meant more for some; in fact, it had meant a day off.

But now, with the polling-place at their door, there were those who could not be bothered to record their votes. After all, they reasoned, would it make any difference. With perhaps justifiable fatalism, they felt certain that their rates and taxes would continue to increase no matter what they did.

The foreshore was a universal dumping-ground. The Council decided to clean it. They tackled the matter energetically. All combustible matter was collected and burnt.

There remained tons of rusty iron, ranging in size and variety from condensed milk tins to discarded iron bedsteads and kitchen ranges. Bones littered the shore. No, there was no mass-murderer about, but there had been a butcher's slaughterhouse.

A path was made round the foreshore. Rusty iron, bones, broken crockery, and every unsightly non-living object which refused to burn was buried under it. " The path to nowhere," sang a local bard. He was wrong. The path led to a hill upon which the Council later placed a seat. For seats were the next benefit to be provided.

These seats, made of green painted wood, with ornamental cast iron ends, had the words, " KYLE

COUNCIL," painted on them. It may be that this gave offence to some wandering cow—or its owner—for within a short period all were broken.

The explanation was believed to be that the animal in scratching herself had entangled her horns between the wooden bars, and had smashed the seat in her efforts to get free. All the seats were broken in a very short time, so the cow must have wandered about a bit. Besides, she must have suffered from a very persistent itch !

Although the Kyle Council was only a voluntary body, it was consulted by the County Council regarding such matters as roads and housing. The Government treated it with due respect. On one occasion when a warship anchored in the bay, representatives were invited on board and entertained. Mr. Anderson shone on such an occasion.

A captured German gun was presented to the Council. It was a bit on the small side, and a wooden stand had to be made for it. It was then placed in front of the Commercial Bank, this being the most imposing and only castellated building. At first I think Mr. Hosack used to take it indoors on wet days ! Eventually it found a resting-place on the balcony of the Kyle Hotel.

I have mentioned some of the successful schemes which the Council tackled. There were others. One was a proposal to introduce electric light. Mr. Mackenzie had been in communication with several firms, and a special meeting was held to consider the correspondence.

It was a cold evening. Mr. Anderson arrived late and sat by the fireside. Mr. Hosack was reading a letter. He paused.

" What is a watt ? " he asked, " You will know, Mr. Anderson".

" Of course I know," said Mr. Anderson, rousing himself. " Let me see now, a watt is a—er —er, dear me, I know perfectly. In fact I have two books at home telling all about watts. I'll go for them."

Mr. Anderson went off for the books, but he encountered some old friends, and the meeting was nearly ended when he returned—bookless and hatless, but full of spirit. Yet a local journalist reported that when he came back he read the Life of James Watt.

Mr. Fraser was the first councillor we lost. I don't think he ever got over that election night in the cart. The whole Council attended the funeral. The day was wet and dreary. We assembled on the railway pier as the remains were placed on board a steam drifter, to be taken by sea to Clachan Duich.

There was a coal strike at the time. Food and supplies were scarce, trains were uncertain. The minister, remembering conditions at home, saw his opportunity. The boat would be passing his Manse. Standing on the pier high above, he shouted down to the skipper below :
" Half a ton of coals."

Mr. Chapman, our missionary, stood beside me. I turned to him and whispered. As I did so, I noticed his face twitching strangely ; yet I had merely asked, " Have they got to take supplies with them ? "

There were still some in the village who preferred the old method by which their committees had been elected. In the past, any budding dictator could have been put on numberless committees by the simple expedient of arranging for someone to nominate him.

The election of the Kyle Council by ballot had been an innovation, and one particularly distasteful to the unsuccessful candidates who did not again offer their services. In the circumstances it was not found to be practicable to hold further elections ; and when vacancies occurred, new members were co-opted. Democracy had been tried and had failed !

Mr. William Shearer, engine-driver, was one of the first members to be co-opted. A noted dancer, he was particularly interested in sports of all kinds. He organised an annual Children's Sports Day, which was very popular. Such a day cannot be chosen far in advance, for our weather is uncertain.

On one occasion he held the sports on a day which some considered unsuitable. His critics—the usual type— lacked energy to help but had ample vitality for criticism. Mr. Shearer had worked hard to make the games a success. He turned on the disgruntled ones ; he told them that, instead of finding fault, they ought to be thanking him. The critics were silenced. They, like sheep before Shearer, were dumb !

The Council functioned for a number of years, carrying out improvements to the satisfaction of some and the confusion of others. It was found that, with a voluntary system, the cost of public benefits was shared unequally. For instance, the street lights shone indiscriminately on subscribers and non-subscribers to the funds.

The Council decided to put forward Mr. Murchison to represent the village on the Parish Council and County Council, statutory bodies empowered to levy rates. Popular with everyone, Mr. Murchison was duly elected. He succeeded during his term of office in helping forward many movements, such as the formation of a nursing association and the appointment of a district nurse. He also initiated action which eventually resulted in the street lighting being paid for out of the rates.

At the time of Mr. Murchison's successful election, I also offered my services as a Parish Councillor ; but with admirable self-denial the electors did not avail themselves of this wonderful opportunity.

No, decidedly no, as was shewn by the result of the poll.   Although unsuccessful, I considered it my duty to thank my supporters ; accordingly I put up a notice, thanking " the 38 intelligent electors " who had voted for me.

Alas, my courtesy was misconstrued.   One lady was deeply offended.   She complained to a friend about me.

" Does he think I am not intelligent ? " she demanded, indignantly.

9

THE SPAR CAVE

DURING many years spent at the Gateway to Skye, I was to visit most parts of the island at different times and under varying conditions. In the early days road transport was limited and rudimentary. My first trip across the island was to Elgol, fifteen miles beyond Broadford.

Mr. Downie, in course of his duties as fishery officer, had occasion to visit that district, and he asked me, along with my wife and children, to accompany him. For there were now two small Macphersons, still lacking in size and years but full of misdirected energy.

After crossing the ferry we all squeezed into an ancient Ford which our driver, an incorrigible humorist, insisted

KYLEAKIN, FROM THE WEST

on calling a car. Away we bumped and heaved, with a considerable amount of clatter, through the village of Kyleakin and on towards Broadford.

Our road lay over miles of undulating moorland upon which a few sad-looking sheep were grazing. We reached Lusa, four miles distant, where the old road to Kylerhea, at one time the main outlet from Skye, branched off.

Down below near the shore stood a lone dwelling, and near it a walled enclosure about three feet high. This was a fank or sheep-fold. There are many such throughout the island, and the town-bred visitor or amateur antiquarian should not mistake them for the ruins of ancient duns.

A sheep farm in Skye is often many miles in extent. At shearing-time the shepherd sends his dogs to scour the mountains and bring in the flock. Again, when the lambs are old enough, the sheep and lambs are herded into the fank, the lambs separated, and the ewes classified. The fank is also used at dipping-time and when the sheep are to be sent away for wintering.

Sheep which remain all the year round on the island are subject to a malady which carries off a number of them. It is found that when year-old ewes are sent away for the winter months, the mortality is relatively small. Besides, turnips are not generally grown in Skye and hand-feeding is very expensive.

So, each autumn, great flocks of sheep cross the ferry at Kyleakin, to be sent east by special train. They remain in the " Low Country " all winter, returning to improved pasture in the spring.

We looked in vain for the tree upon which Saint Maelrubha had hung his bell when he came to preach the gospel a thousand years ago. According to tradition, this bell rang of its own volition as required.

The disappearance of the tree was probably due to the need for firewood. For coal fires have now replaced peat in many homes, and wood is required for kindling. It was otherwise when a peat fire burnt continuously on every hearth. In those days, before retiring to rest, the housewife covered the dying embers with ashes and in the morning removed the ashes and resuscitated the fire.

Beyond Lusa lay Breakish, a crofting township which surprised me as it has amazed others. Instead of primitive dwellings, such as one saw in many rural parts not only of the Highlands but of the " enlightened " Lowlands, we found that the dwelling-houses were all comparatively modern. Each house was a two-storey building with slated roof.

I learnt that many of these houses had been rebuilt or renovated with money sent from abroad by kinsmen. Sons had been compelled to emigrate to America or Australia in order to earn a livelihood. But Skye was still their home, as it would be counted the home of their descendants.

The scenery became mountainous as we approached the village of Broadford. Behind it rose Beinn-na-Caillich, a mountain of the same name as the one above Kyleakin. *Cailleach* is the Gaelic for " old woman." Each Ben lays claim to having had an elderly Norwegian princess buried on its summit several centuries ago.

Blaven, nearby, makes a similar claim. And why not ? Those were the days of large families, and no doubt princesses were plentiful.

We turned west at Broadford and proceeded along Glen Suardel past the ruins of the church where Saint

Maelrubha came with his bell and his message. But the bell, which he had taken from its tree at Ashaig, refused to ring in its new environment.

On the hillside stood gaunt empty buildings connected with the marble quarries which had been in active operation for a few years, but which had been closed before the outbreak of the Great War. The marble, although not quarried to any great extent, was known centuries ago. It was used for mantelpieces in Armadale Castle, built in the beginning of the nineteenth century.

Our road lay round Kilchrist Loch, an uninviting piece of water. Beyond it a cart track branched south to Suishnish and continued westward to Boreraig. These were once populous townships where men and women lived and worked and reared their children.

But they were not permitted to die there, for an unprincipled factor, serving a weak master, had them evicted.

These crofts had been reclaimed from the moors by their occupants or their ancestors. Their rudely-built dwellings had been erected by themselves. But these considerations did not count when, eighty years ago, ten families were driven from these townships.

An English-bred chieftain, ignorant of conditions, was easily persuaded by a crafty factor that it was in the true interests of the people to emigrate. Skye was becoming overcrowded. Generous chief, he would send them to Canada where there was more room for them.

So these two townships became one large sheep farm, and in due course the minister, a friend of the factor, became the tenant. He had preached resignation and obedience to his flock. He reaped his earthly reward.

We passed Torrin, a larger and more scattered

township at the base of Ben Dearg. Here we got a splendid view of Blaven, with its jagged outline, and Glamaig and Marsco in the distance. The peaceful waters of Loch Slapin were spread out before us. Our road skirted the shore, near which several Highland cattle were standing, flicking their tails.

Farther on we passed Strathaird House, at one time the home of the Chiefs of Mackinnon. Below, near the shore, lay Kilmaree Churchyard, dedicated to Saint Maelrubha.

The road ascended along the side of Ben Meabost to a height of over a thousand feet. Below us were indications of a track, now grass-covered, which had led to Glasnakille. Across Loch Slapin and Loch Eishort stretched the whole peninsula of Sleat, with the hills of Knoydart on the mainland beyond.

Elgol is another scattered township. We halted at the house of Mrs. Mackinnon, below which a precipitous road led down to the shore. I was told that on two recent occasions motorists had ventured down the road, only to find they were unable to return unaided. The ascent had only been possible with the assistance of cart horses. Now the County Council had erected a board with a warning notice.

Our journey of twenty-three miles had occupied fully two hours, and we were grateful for the cup of refreshing tea which Mrs. Mackinnon thoughtfully provided. Neil, my little boy of a year old, was delighted with the old lady who spoke to him in Gaelic and called him a " bodachan beg" (a little old man).

Elgol appeared to be fairly populous. Much of the land was cultivated, mostly in small fields or patches. Some of the houses were quite modern, although there were still many black ones. These so-called " black " houses had low-built walls and thatched roof common to all, but they varied in other respects. Some, to put it mildly, were past their best ; but others were very picturesque, clean, and inviting.

I have actually heard men and women express wonder at people living in such places. How could they bear the peat reek ? Surely the smoke of a peat is less poisonous than that of the weed which is almost universally smoked to-day.

As for the cleanliness of peat, don't we find wealthy women going to Strathpeffer to bathe in peat slime ? But of course these ladies are taking the " cure " which happens to be the latest fad of their fashionable specialist.

What if there was an old herring barrel on the top of some dwelling for a chimney ? It served its purpose, and, to the unbiassed observer, seemed less out of place than the crude embellishments seen on some of our public buildings. A case in point (literally) is Marischal College, Aberdeen, where the tips of the granite spires are gilded with gold leaf !

I have also heard criticism of the clay floors in some of the houses. " Dirty," was the description applied by one lady. Did the woman realise what she was saying ? Her own face was, mercifully perhaps, plastered with face powder—actually dried clay, with a smell—and her lips were artificially coloured with the dried bodies of dead insects.

In these humble dwellings at Elgol there lived at that time many God-fearing women who were not afraid or ashamed to shew their faces as their Creator had made them.

From the hill above Mrs. Mackinnon's house a

marvellous view was obtained. In front stretched the Cuillins, their dark serrated peaks sharply outlined against the sky. Across Scavaig and beyond the first low-lying ridge we glimpsed Loch Coruisk, that wonder-loch immortalised by Sir Walter Scott. To the west lay the Isle of Soay, and far out on the horizon the isle of Rum.

Since that day I have seen Skye in varying moods. I have seen it with the rain pouring down, hour after hour, day after day. I have seen it in a wild gale when the wind howled and the storm raged, and it seemed impossible that any man-built shelter could withstand its onslaught.

I have seen it with scorching sun blazing out of azure sky ; when vegetation became parched and burnt, and living creatures became listless and enervated. But never have I beheld a grander scene than Elgol on that glorious, perfect day.

Mr. Downie and I now set out to visit the Spar Cave, which we had been told was near Glasnakille, " a mile or so " across the moor. Mr. Hay, owner-driver of our chariot, acted as guide. He, it seemed, had a better realisation of the length of a Skye mile.

Mr. Hay was a very entertaining companion. He knew everyone in the district and had a tale to tell about most of them. There was the story of Red Angus, a well-known worthy in his day.

One morning, as Angus was working on his croft, he was greatly startled to see a man cycling down the hill. In those days bicycles had fixed wheels, and the cyclist who wished to rest his legs had to place them on foot-rests in front. This one was wearing a long dark overcoat and a bowler hat. The wheels were hidden from view by an intervening wall. In any case, old Angus had never seen a bicycle in his life.

SEA ENTRANCE TO SPAR CAVE

All he now saw was this dark figure skimming along at what he considered to be a miraculous speed. He saw the feet stretched out in front, and the coat-tails trailing in the breeze behind. There could be no doubt as to the identity of the apparition. Rushing to the house, he shouted to his wife, " Morag, Morag, come out this minute and see the Devil, or he'll be at the back of Harris in no time at all".

When we reached Glasnakille, Norman Macdonald very kindly offered to row us to the mouth of the cave. We approached the sea by a path down a wild ravine. The boat was high and dry and required our united strength to drag it down to the sea.

After rowing round several headlands, our boat was headed for an opening between two high cliffs. We entered a narrow gorge at the head of which we disembarked ; then, scrambling over boulders, we climbed to a narrow plateau near the mouth of the cave. Water trickled down upon us. Far above our heads appeared a great gap through which a cold dim light penetrated.

We entered the Spar Cave. Our electric torches shone feebly. Hay and Macdonald carried lanterns which proved more serviceable. We began the ascent of the marble stairway which Nature, during countless centuries, had built. Reaching the top, we passed through an archway formed of mighty pillars. We were in a primeval laboratory.

We listened to the sound of the calcium-impregnated water as it came dripping down from the domed ceiling, invisible in the distance. Around us stretched walls of marble, and beneath our feet the same glistening whiteness. The remains of numerous stalactites hung from above. The stalagmites beneath had mostly disappeared.

F

Vandals—the same type who tear up wild flowers—had removed these marvels, probably to discard them later.

The cave sloped downward, a pool of clear water barring our further progress. Sir Walter Scott, in the " Lord of the Isles," describes it as,

> " The mermaid's alabaster grot
>   Who bathes her limbs in sunless well,
>   Deep in Strathaird's enchanted cell."

The cave is also known as Slochd Altrimen, or the Nursling Cave. According to tradition, the Princess Dounhuila, daughter of the king of Ulster, secretly married to young Colonsay, hid her child in this cave where it was guarded by Colonsay's dog. In such a wet place the poor child must have badly needed its grandfather's Ulster !

We were unable to cross the crystal pool ; but were assured that, beyond it, a passage continued far into the mountain. Into this passage a MacCrimmon, piper to the Chief of Macleod, is said to have marched, playing his pipes full blast, and been lost for ever.

No reason has been given for MacCrimmon's march ; not even a suggestion that his music was so unpopular that he went to escape his victims. Taking into consideration the clan to which he belonged and the times in which he lived, I hazard the opinion that the cave contained a secret still. Anyhow the end of MacCrimmon is a secret, still.

10

A DAY IN THE PHARMACY

THE day started badly. I arrived several minutes
late, to find a crusty customer waiting impatiently.
"Sorry to keep you waiting," I said. He grunted.
I went on cheerily, determined to make the best of the
situation, "Patience is a virtue."

He glared.

"And so is punctuality," he snapped back. I was
not surprised when he asked for a box of liver pills.

A sweet young creature now tripped daintily in. She
looked around, and appeared to be in no hurry—probably
her friend was late and she had to pass the time somehow.

"So nice to find a chemist here," she chirped. "I
don't suppose you stock Madame Pomeroy's Skin Food?"

"Oh, yes," I answered, reaching prematurely for the
article mentioned.

"Do you really?" she said, evidently slightly taken
aback, "I did not think you would be likely to have it.
Well, —er, —er, I have some at present, but will know
where to get more if I need it. Good morning."

Several equally unremunerative customers followed.
One boy wanted a free box for a rabbit-hutch, another
needed change for a sixpence, and a "lost" woman
desired to be directed to the ferry. Mr. Humphrey came
with a notice to be exhibited in a window.

Mr. John Humphrey is group scoutmaster, a most
energetic and enthusiastic one. Incidentally, he is head
booking-clerk at the railway station. Some years ago he

planned leaving the district, and the people at once decided to make a public presentation to him.

An appeal for subscriptions met with a ready response, and the day of the presentation arrived. It was a great occasion. There was a large gathering of friends. Speeches were made, eulogising the virtues and good qualities of our departing townsman. Touching tributes were paid to his zeal for the Scouts and his helpfulness to the whole community.

Surely not till then had Mr. Humphrey realised that he possessed all the virtues and that he had none of the vices to which weaker men are addicted. His voice quivering with emotion, he thanked his fellow-townsmen for their beautiful words, their generous appreciation, but above all for the gift of a handsome clock.

Could he find it in his heart to part with a people who were so fond of him ? No, most emphatically, no. So to-day the clock still goes, but Mr. Humphrey remains.

There was a brief lull ; then through the open doorway appeared a bevy of young men and women talking, laughing, and gesticulating. The *Claymore*, a pleasure cruiser from Glasgow, had just arrived with a hundred passengers on board.

A seething mass filled the limited space in the pharmacy, while others waited their turn outside. Business became brisk. Sunglasses, face cream, sun-burn lotion, books, post-cards, all were in demand. A spool for this customer, a bottle of Eno for the next, and so on. Some of the visitors had been up on previous cruises, and it was a mutual pleasure to meet again. A busy hour passed quickly.

The postman now arrived. My old friend, Sandy Post, no longer a " Government slave "—to use his own description—had inherited a coal-merchant's business in Dingwall. So Sandy had left us. He found sacks of coal more profitable than sacks of mails.

Last time I saw Sandy in Kyle, he had been attending the funeral of a relative. His face beamed as we shook hands.

" We've all got to go when our time comes," he said, cheerily.

This morning the mails were brought by his successor, Mr. Donald Mackinnon, popularly known as Donald the Post. He served with distinction in the Great War and came to us after demobilisation. Now he is one of our busiest townsmen.

In intervals of delivering letters, Donald will cut your hair, regulate your clock, or overhaul your motor-cycle or car. He invented a twine-saving device for use in post offices, and received in return not only the Postmaster-General's thanks but also a cheque, microscopic in amount but nevertheless welcome.

On this particular morning Donald wanted three-pence for a letter which had been posted unpaid the previous evening. Interest at the rate of one hundred per cent. per day—or thirty-six thousand five hundred per cent. per annum—had been added !

One letter, addressed to me personally, began, " Dear Sir or Madam." This seemed a bit unkind, even if I did wear my hair unfashionably long. Perhaps it was merely my correspondent's idea of how to begin a business letter.

The next asked for, " A box of pills for removing the bowels ! " Too bad to smile, my customer did not want a surgical operation. He was probably thinking in one language and writing in another, and a mistake in trans-lation might easily occur.

Among other letters was one from a dear old lady of ninety-four who lived alone in a crofting township about fifty miles distant. She had told me her age in a letter some time previously. She sent the address of her son— a young fellow about seventy—in case she died leaving anything unpaid. Honest soul, she always sent a remittance very promptly.

This morning she wrote rather despondently, stating that she was not feeling so well as usual. Then she added, in simple language yet in words so full of pathos, " I am a very old woman."

Another letter was also from a woman, but not an old one. She would not grow old in years. She was waiting, hopefully, to die.

I read the prescription. I unlocked the cupboard door with the skull and cross-bones painted on it, and I measured out the required quantity of her drug. She would require larger and yet larger doses. For months, perhaps even a year or two, she might linger, with brief periods of relief from pain. . . . We would not let a dog suffer so.

I had just got all orders ready for despatch by post, and was preparing to go to luncheon, when Miss Mackinnon appeared with her dog Ossian. As a Macpherson, I felt I had a proprietary interest in a dog bearing such a distinguished name !

Besides, I was always glad to see Miss Mackinnon. Although most of our community had their mid-day meal at this hour, she was different. Living alone, I fancy her meal hours were regulated more by the state of her digestion than by a clock.

The last of the Mackinnons of Skye, she was directly descended from the Chief of Mackinnon who had befriended

Prince Charles Edward Stuart. She now lived in a small cottage in our village where she could gaze across the narrow waters to her old home at Kyle House among the trees.

When quite a young girl she had spent some time in India. There she had met and dined with the late Lord Roberts when he was a junior officer. She could tell a good story. When she first visited India, she would greet her friends with, " Another beautiful morning." Then she noticed that this " wasn't done " in India, where beautiful mornings were accepted as a matter of course.

On this occasion she had called to shew me a letter she had received from a friend in London. Her correspondent wrote—in good time, for it was still summer—telling her that if she intended sending a post-card next Christmas she might select a different view. It appeared that for four consecutive years Miss Mackinnon had sent her friend a photograph of the Five Sisters of Kintail !

After a hurried meal I returned in time for the arrival of the afternoon train. Housewives from Duirinish, Plockton, and Stromeferry frequently travelled by this train. They came carrying baskets of eggs and butter which they disposed of at the Pioneer Stores ; returning home by the five o'clock train laden with provisions, crockery, clothing, and even bags of flour and oatmeal.

Soon there came a stream of passengers off the train. Several called to replace articles they had left behind, the most frequent request being for a toothbrush. One young man came in search of a shaving outfit.

This young man had just discovered that there was no hairdresser in the place. Poor youth, he had never shaved himself. He had left the so-called civilisation of the city, and already he was miserable. But his holiday would do him good ; he would go back, thankful to be home again. It was unlikely that he would return to the Highlands, but he might derive pleasure from sending some of his friends there.

There was a brief lull during which I had time to glance at a newspaper. It was a daily national paper which, despite its sensational tone, varied little in essentials from day to day. There were the usual reports of society weddings, murder trials, divorce court proceedings, and international complications. I should have to wait until the week-end before the local weekly appeared. In it there would be the really " important " news, the names of the artistes at the previous week's concert, the M.C.s at the dance which followed, and, of course, a list of the ladies who poured out the tea at the Young Women's Guild.

The doctor now came breezily in. Dr. MacRae is our parish doctor—a very capable, hard-working one. He is responsible for the maintenance of good health in the parishes of Lochalsh, Glenshiel, and Kintail, an area which has the services of eight ministers, one priest, and two missionaries to look after its spiritual welfare.

The doctor is not supposed to need sleep. Day and night he is expected to be at the beck and call of every dipsomaniac, hypochondriac, and neurotic crank. Even his meal hours are believed to be arranged not for his own sustenance but so that visiting patients may know when to find him at home.

Yet our doctor manages to find time to preside at concerts and meetings. I remember one concert where the doctor was in the chair. A perspiring damsel had made the rafters ring with her perfervid rendering of " Danny Boy." The doctor stood up as she finished.

" I guess Danny heard that all right," he remarked.

The doctor is equally popular at a political meeting. He was the genial chairman at a recent parliamentary by-election. One of the candidates was holding a meeting in the Public Hall. It was a Saturday night, and some of those in the back of the hall became noisy.

" A little less noise from the screw-tops," called out the doctor, hinting at the probable origin of their restless-ness. But the rebuked ones had not been slow to notice the anti-tee-total composition of the platform party.

" Look after the screw-tops beside you, doctor," came the instant reply.

This afternoon the doctor had just gone when an excursion train from Inverness and Elgin arrived. The road from the station, after crossing the railway, slopes downwards to the pharmacy. Along this road now came several hundred excursionists.

Down towards me and swiftly past, they marched full speed, the smaller ones occasionally breaking into a run, all eagerly bound for the ferry. A few stout or elderly ones, or perhaps those of more philosophic mould, brought up the rear.

Two motor-boats were waiting at the ferry, but these were capable of carrying only a fraction of their number at a time. Several trips were necessary before all got across.

Kyleakin is an interesting village, but few day excursionists have time to admire it. Indeed, no sooner do they land there than they find they have to return almost immediately. But not before sending post-cards to their friends ! That is a rite—no pun intended—which no pilgrim to Skye may neglect.

So these excursionists, like many thousands before

them, posted their cards on the Island in the belief that the magic words, " Isle of Skye," would appear on the post-mark.

Vain hope and wasted effort ! They had not reckoned with the intricate working of the Post Office. That admirable institution believes in efficiency but has no place for sentiment—unless it can charge extra for it, as in the case of a Greetings telegram.

So it is that Kyleakin, although geographically in the Isle of Skye, Inverness-shire, is nevertheless, for postal purposes, Kyleakin, Kyle, Ross-shire.

Fearful of being stranded in the isle of their dreams, the crowd early began to return. For a short time they wandered along the Main Street of our village. Some bought souvenirs to take back ; others went in search of food. Soon all found their way back to the railway station.

After the departure of the excursion train the village settled down to its usual evening quiet, re-awakening for a brief period on the arrival of the last train from the east.

The evening train is popular with those visitors from Glasgow or Edinburgh who believe in starting the day at a reasonable hour. Of course, there are cranks who prefer to leave home at the unearthly hour of four or five in the morning, in order to reach Kyle in the early afternoon. Such people spend the remainder of the day grumbling because the only newspapers procurable are those they have already read.

This evening there was not only an unusually large number of visitors, but there were several " commercials." Among the latter was my old friend, Mr. J. A. Ross, from Aberdeen.

I remember Mr. Ross when I was a boy, and he looks

as youthful as ever, although his hearing is not now so good. But partial deafness has advantages. Mr. Ross has much writing to do at night, and in a hotel writing-room, where young bloods are relating more or less veracious tales, he can proceed peacefully with his work.

Arriving at Kyle of Lochalsh, as he usually does, by the evening train, he will reach his hotel in time for dinner. But Mr. Ross refuses to dine at night.

" I take my dinner in the middle of the day," he will inform the waiter. " Bring me some supper."

Although not a big man, he refuses to be put off with a small bedroom where, as he puts it, " You couldn't swing a cat."

In the morning he will be up early and ready to transact business. When he goes away he will take with him a cheque—for Mr. Ross has a hopeful, trusting personality—and will hand me a receipt. As he puts the matter succinctly,

" You give me one piece of paper, and I give you another."

This evening, Mr. Ross, after a cheery greeting, went off to his hotel, supper, and telephone. Business could wait.

The last customer had gone. The day's labours were ended. I set out up the village street, past Mr. MacGregor's Tweed Shop and along by the Old Institute.

Rory Bagdad and Big Willie were having a friendly chat, talking over old times, their backs to the waters of Pladaig Bay, oblivious to the beauty of the dying sun over Raasay. And beauty less remote appeared to interest the boys playing cricket on the railway playing-field nearby, while the village belles looked interestedly on.

I turned along the narrow way and climbed the

difficult road to my brown heather-clad hill with its modest cottage. Here were home, the garden, and the midges.

II

PILGRIMAGE TO KILMUIR

MR. DONALD SKINNER, at that time the pro-gressive proprietor of the King's Arms Hotel, Kyleakin, may be regarded as the pioneer of motor-omnibus tours in Skye. His was the first char-a-banc to run trips to the various beauty spots and historic places on the island.

He had a number of difficulties to overcome. There was as yet no telephone service between Skye and the mainland. So a code of signals was arranged in order that passengers from Kyle might have seats reserved for them when they crossed the ferry.

Thus any fine morning during the tourist season Mr. Skinner might have been observed, telescope to eye, gazing across to the mainland. He was searching the blackboard for the number of passengers booked. Another board beside him supplied similar information to his colleague at Kyle.

Mr. Skinner was very proud of his first char-a-banc. Before putting it into regular service he decided upon a trial trip. Along with him and several others, I set out on that historic run.

We were perched high on the open vehicle, receiving the full blast of the wild moorland breezes. We climbed hills at five miles an hour and went spinning down the other side at twenty.

On we sped, past Lusa and Breakish, to Broadford. Here the Elgol road branches to the left, and to the right a narrow road leads to the steamboat pier.

Our road stretched straight ahead. Corry was on our right, hidden among trees. We had not proceeded far before we saw a long dark procession approaching. We halted as it drew near.

An old man, living alone up the glen, had died ; and every man, old and young, had turned out to pay his last tribute, and to assist in carrying the body to its final resting-place. Even to-day, when customs are slowly changing, the use of a hearse is looked upon with disfavour.

A Skye funeral is an impressive sight. The men march in front in military formation. Then follows the coffin, resting on a bier, borne along by eight mourners. The near relatives bring up the rear. As the procession marches along, four men step out at certain intervals from the ranks at either side. These take the place of the bearers who go forward to the front.

There are several halting-places by the wayside where the coffin is rested while the company partakes of refreshments. In the old days a horse and cart accompanied the cortege with a supply of whisky, bread, and, cheese. Now this is seldom seen.

There is a story told of a time when Highlanders were not all quite so sober as to-day. The home of the departed was many miles from the burial place, and mourners were fewer than usual. After a time it was decided to put the coffin in the cart. At each halting-place it was removed while refreshments were brought out.

The halts were many ; and it was late in the evening when the funeral party, marching solemnly behind the cart, at last reached the churchyard. All was in readiness. Alas, the cart held only an empty jar. The coffin had been left by the wayside.

Beyond Corry the road stretched over moor and hill, then dipped down to the sea opposite Scalpay island. Captain Muntz is the present owner of the islands of Scalpay, Pabay, and Longay. His neighbouring proprietor, Captain Shaw of Corry, vouches for the authenticity of the following conversation which took place between the two lairds.

Scalpay : Can you tell me where I can buy a horse ? My present one is getting too old.

Corry : What do you want with a horse ?   You have no work for one.

Scalpay : Oh, I need a horse to bring in the hay.

Corry : And what do you need hay for ?

Scalpay : To feed the horse.

The road branched left at Strollamus, past Black Donald's Cave. Donald was black of hair and black of heart. Drovers who came his way with their cattle would invariably miss a cow or calf, always the best of their drove. Donald Dubh had ensnared the animals with a noose made of horse hair.

He was suspected at last and would have been apprehended but contrived to escape. He left behind him his wife and grown-up son. The officers of the law came questioning these and forced the son to reveal how the captures had been made. When Black Donald heard this, he swore to kill his son.

The mother sent her son away for safety. He walked along Strath Mor, and had reached the rising ground between the two lochs when his father, creeping up behind, struck him dead. To this day, I have been assured, people passing the fatal spot feel a gust of ice-cold air. And few will go this way after dark.

The road sloped upwards above Dunan, a crofting township spread out along the shore with, apparently, no definite road access. We approached the sea again at Luib, another pleasing old-world hamlet lying at the head of Loch Ainort.

A strange incident occurred at a *ceilidh* held in one of the houses here. Many people had gathered in the cottage one evening. They were talking, laughing, telling stories, and singing. Suddenly Lachlan Mackinnon, a widower who had lost his wife a year previously, saw a " vision."

Lachlan saw a woman seated in the midst of the company, although no woman was there. He had never seen the face before. Yet he knew, with that curious knowledge which people acquire in dreams, that this was the face of his future wife.

Some months later a strange woman came to reside in the district. Lachlan recognised her as the woman of his " vision." In due course she became his wife. It had to be !

We crossed the old bridge at the foot of Drum nam Cleochd. Here the char-a-banc was halted and we all got out. We had to walk up the steep rough road, for our driver was taking no risks on that perilous hillside. The day was remarkably fine, but we could imagine the discomfort if it had been wet.

For Skye weather is thorough. A shower seldom lasts less than an hour, and as often as not continues the whole day. Then the dark clouds cover the mountains while the rain pours steadily down; and the wind, howling through the glens and corries, drives piercingly through every article of clothing until one is drenched to the skin.

But Skye rain does not hurt, and when it clears there is ample compensation. After each rainfall a thousand tiny rivulets come to life, and the mountain streams become raging torrents as they dash down the dark gorges.

Then the sun appears and scatters the mists encircling the cloud-capped peaks. In a moment the dull leaden sky is clear, and the clouds, rising and scattering, breaking and uniting, produce myriads of shapes and forms, and finally their insubstantial pageant fades leaving not a wrack behind.

After our steep climb we were glad to find our conveyance waiting at the top of the hill. We should have to get out again and walk down the hill on our return journey, but we were not yet aware of that pleasure in store.

The road now lay along a stretch of wild glen, in the shadow of the mountain peaks. It was interesting to observe how the passengers reacted to the beauty of the scene.

Two ladies, in particular, had just discovered mutual acquaintances. They talked. Oh, how they talked! Then one would suddenly break off.

" Isn't that hill lovely ? " she would say.

" Yes, charming," the other would reply, giving a cursory glance at the object in question, then continuing animatedly,

" And so you know the Browns."

They were off again. The glories of mountain and

glen, the wonders of loch and sky were lost upon them.
Not of them did Byron write :

> " Are not the mountains, waves and skies a part
> Of me and of my soul, as I of them ? "

Ahead of us grey Glamaig towered high, with the
winding river below. Along this silent way had come the
Prince for whom our ancestors had been proud to fight.
Here he had wandered, singing and whistling, a price on
his head.

We reached the sea again near Sconser. A shooting-
lodge now stood where the old inn had been. Clanranald
had met the Skye Chiefs here in 1745. He had hoped for
support for the Prince. But they failed him, as they were
later to fail their clansmen.

Opposite Sconser the isle of Raasay stood out boldly,
separated from Skye by the Narrows and Kyle More.
The road curved westward round the base of Glamaig.
Below were the calm waters of Loch Sligachan, an arm of
the sea stretching several miles inland. Across the loch
lay the historic crofting township of Braes, the scene of
the famous " battle " which occurred in 1882.

Here a handful of crofters, unable to pay rent, were
proceeded against by the sheriff-officer at Portree. This
officer, a man named Martin, was an inefficient, humorless
clod. The crofters tore the summons out of his hands and
burned it. In the quaint language of Scots law, the
officer had been deforced.

The authorities decided to punish the " crime " and
to arrest the " criminal." Their own police force proving
inadequate for the purpose, they succeeded by some
underground method in persuading Glasgow City Police
to send assistance. Accordingly, fifty brawny members
of that body, armed with revolvers, were brought to Skye.

G

Those brave stalwarts, accompanied by members of Inverness Constabulary and supported by two sheriffs and two fiscals, marched out from Portree. They would teach these poor ill-clad, undernourished crofters a lesson !

It was early morning, a time at which we in the west are not at our best. The men of the Braes were taken by surprise, and in a short time five suspects were arrested.

Pandemonium broke loose. Every conceivable kind of missile was thrown at the invaders ; pieces of wood, anything movable, all were hurled at the alien horde.

Maledictions were showered upon the heads of Martin and the equally detested factor. They and their children —they probably had none, but when the Celt is wound up he does not let such a trifle cramp his style—were fervently cursed.

The English language proving too feeble for the purpose, recourse was had to the more virile Gaelic, from which pleasant tongue I translate the following :

" Cursed be you and yours for ten generations and to all eternity."

"May the red haired factor find a place in the hottest part of Ifrinn ! "

The police had to take their prisoners to Portree. The road, a mere cattle track, lay through a gully. From the heights above, men and women rolled down huge boulders, regardless of the fact that the prisoners were as likely to be hit as their captors.

Twelve Skye policemen were injured, several seriously, before the prisoners were lodged safely in Portree prison. Next day they were taken to Inverness where they were tried and trifling fines imposed.

Although no money had been available for payment

of rent, it is noteworthy that the fines were promptly paid. The heroes of the Braes returned home triumphant. The Battle of the Braes was over.

But the rents were still unpaid. Something must be done. It might curtail the London season for the Highland landowners if crofters all over the Highlands were to withhold payment. There would be no money to squander in London. And no Englishman would tolerate their uncouth manners for any other reason !

Another appeal was made for police assistance. Glasgow had learnt its lesson ; it refused to send more men. Edinburgh, Greenock, and Paisley were next appealed to, and they also refused. Indeed, the finest of the men in these forces were Highlanders, and they had no desire to take part in this petty persecution of their kinsmen.

It was pitiful to see this wretched factor scouring Scotland in vain for help against the crofters. The bungling fool made his employer a laughing-stock throughout the country.

Lord MacDonald was the owner of the Braes. Although an absentee landowner, as was the fashion of his day, he was the lineal descendant of the great Chiefs of the MacDonalds, Lords of the Isles.

These men had held their lands for many centuries, held them for themselves and their clansmen ; clansmen who had shared their joys and sorrows, clansmen who would have died for them.

At the head of the loch stands Sligachan Hotel, a noted resort for climbers and anglers. In the foreground the river sweeps beneath the old stone bridge ; and behind, the peaks of Sgurr nan Gillean rise majestically.

The path to Harta Corrie and Loch Coruisk stretches up the south bank of the river. Along this way many thousands of tourists have gone, on foot or by hill pony, to see the famous loch. Across the bridge the road branches. To the left it leads to Glenbrittle, Carbost, and Dunvegan.

We proceeded northward along Glen Varragill, a wide expanse of barren, lonely moorland. On our right rose Ben Lee, and on our left flowed the River Varragill, fed by gushing rivulets and turbulent waterfalls.

An inlet of Portree Bay flowed south to meet us. The waters of the loch lay smooth and motionless on their black rocky bed. Near the shore on a tiny islet were the ruins of a church, one of several in Skye dedicated to Saint Columba.

We turned westward as we approached Portree, passing on the outskirts of the town some dilapidated black houses which have since been demolished. At Borve, some miles farther on, we held north, again approaching the sea at Kensaleyre near the head of Loch Snizort.

We reached the road leading to Kingsburgh where I left the party in order to explore the historic place. At the entrance to Kingsburgh House I was fortunate in meeting the proprietor, a very courteous Highlander ; though, to my Jacobite eyes, he was strangely out of place in this ancient home of the MacDonalds.

For the Prince, a fugitive, had come to Kingsburgh House where he had slept in safety. Here MacDonald of Kingsburgh and Mrs. MacDonald had entertained the son of their king. And now, here a modern Kingsburgh stood, and his kilt was of the Campbell tartan.

The present house is nicely situated near the wooded

shore. Scarcely a trace remains of the old historic building. Even the stones of its walls have been carried off as souvenirs, many to the other side of the Atlantic.

Kingsburgh directed me to the well, down by the river bank, where the Prince had rested on his journey from Monkstadt. I found it in a secluded hollow, probably little changed with the passing of centuries. The well was merely a round hole in the ground, with the clear water bubbling up. There was no drinking-cup, no stone to mark the passing of the Royal visitor.

I knelt by the well and drank.

Continuing our tour northward we passed, a mile farther on, the ruins of Caisteal Uisdean, or Hugh's Castle. Hugh MacDonald, presumably gifted with second sight like many of his race and foreseeing the imposition of a window-tax, built his castle entirely without windows. The only access was by a door high up on the wall.

He spent much of his time in plotting the death of his kinsman, Donald Gorme. Unfortunately for Hugh, the great mind of Donald Gorme was similarly occupied. He succeeded in tempting Hugh from his lair, persuading him to go to Duntulm Castle as his guest.

But the honoured guest no sooner entered the castle than he was thrown into a dungeon. There he was fed on salt meat and slowly starved to death.

We continued north through the populous district of Earlish and on to Uig where the road rises high above the bay. A circular tower on our left aroused curiosity. An elderly man with a soured, disillusioned look on his face, was sitting by the roadside. We halted, and I enquired as to the origin and purpose of the tower.

The tired one got to his feet. He looked me slowly up and down. Next he tried me with " the Gaelic " ;

then, concluding that I was a miserable Lowlander and could therefore swallow anything, he began his tale. Briefly, this was his story :

" There once lived in Uig an old man who was married to a young woman. She was flighty and for ever gadding about. So the old man built this tower, with windows all round. No matter which way his wife went, he could keep watch."

My informant did not explain what happened when the wife disappeared round a corner.

The actual facts, as I have since learnt, were even less interesting. The tower was merely a dwelling-house built by the proprietor, Captain Frazer of Newton, in this particular shape to add interest to the landscape.

Forty years before my visit, Lord MacDonald had sold part of the parish of Snizort and the whole of Kilmuir to Captain Frazer. The new proprietor had carried out many improvements. Besides the erection of the tower, he had built a mansion house at the mouth of Glen Uig.

This proved an unfortunate site. Shortly after the house was built a great storm arose causing the River Conon to overflow its banks. A landslide temporarily held up the waters. Then the swollen river, bursting forth with terrific force, swept down, carrying all before it.

It carried away part of the burial ground, a coffin being actually hurled through the back door of the mansion house. The flooded building, unable to stand the pressure, collapsed and was swept out to sea.

Strangely enough, this extraordinary occurrence was not foretold by the Brahan Seer. That worthy prophet, being a Lewisman, probably scorned to use his gifts for the benefit of Skye.

Uig is one of the few fishing centres on the west of

Skye, a considerable quantity of herrings being landed there during a good season. Its long narrow pier stretches a quarter of a mile into the bay. At the shore end a monument commemorates the visit of King Edward VII in 1902.

Beyond the village the road ascends steeply. Our driver had difficulty in negotiating one particularly acute bend. The Stack of Skudiburgh shewed up on our left with the ruins of a dun on a nearby promontory.

We passed the farm road leading to Monkstadt. Down by the shore is the spot where the Prince and Flora MacDonald had landed. No trace now remains of the cave where he rested while Flora went on ahead to spy out the land.

We continued through the crofting township of Kilmuir, known because of its fertile fields as the granary of Skye. In front stretched Score Bay. To the right lay the old churchyard of Kilmuir where once had stood the Church of Saint Mary.

We turned up a narrow road which led past the Manse, a substantial building which has since become the residence of Seton Gordon, the Scottish ornithologist and author. A gale blew fiercely as we approached the churchyard, this ancient burial-place of the Lords of the Isles.

But it was not to visit the resting-places of these forgotten Chiefs that we had come. Like countless thousands before us, we turned towards the grey granite cross. We stood before the tomb of Flora MacDonald, the Skye heroine who had risked her life for the fugitive Prince.

In a later century another prince was to become a wanderer from his native land, and those who had fawned upon him when in power were to be without a kind thought for him in adversity. But it was when Prince Charles Edward Stuart was defeated, penniless, almost hopeless, in the hour of his greatest need, that Flora MacDonald had come to his aid.

And so to-day that great memorial cross stands there, a landmark seen by mariners far out at sea. The words of the inscription are :

FLORA MACDONALD
PRESERVER OF PRINCE CHARLES EDWARD STUART.
HER NAME WILL BE MENTIONED IN HISTORY AND
IF COURAGE AND FIDELITY BE VIRTUES MENTIONED
WITH HONOUR.

12

A TRIP TO APPLECROSS

SAINT MAELRUBHA sailed in his frail coracle to Applecross, on the west coast of Scotland. There, in 673, at the mouth of the River Crossan, he founded the Monastery of Applecross or Abercrossan.

The centuries passed ; and his successor the Reverend Malcolm Laing, M.A., Minister of Applecross, sailed south in a fishing boat to Kyle of Lochalsh, bringing with him his church choir. It was a gala-afternoon at Kyle, where a large gathering had assembled for the opening of the first tennis court.

Mr. Robert MacLeod, postmaster, was president of the Tennis Club. The making of the court had proved costly. It had meant blasting through solid rock, filling up peat bog, carting sand and soil. But Mr. MacLeod

FLORA MACDONALD'S MONUMENT

had come from the most easterly corner of Aberdeenshire. He had excelled in raising funds.

Lady Arthur Cecil performed the opening ceremony and afterwards played in the first match. Our guests from Applecross had to go back early to suit the tide. Otherwise they might have delayed their return, for Mr. Laing at this time was unmarried and his choir was not wholly a male voice one. But I digress.

He very kindly invited me to accompany him back to Applecross. At this time my wife and family were spending a holiday in Lewis. As they would be returning from Stornoway by the *Shiela* next morning, I could join their boat when it called at Applecross Bay on the way south. So I gladly accepted.

It was early on that delightful June evening when, along with Mr. Laing and his church choir, I got on board the fishing boat. It had not been fitted out as a pleasure cruiser, and each one of us had to find a box, a coil of rope or, as Dr. Johnson might have said, some other protuberance. At length we all settled down as comfortably as circumstances permitted.

Away we sailed, beyond the Plock of Kyle and past the lighthouse. It was thrilling at first but soon became monotonous. On we sailed. The boat heaved and rolled. The evening became colder and colder. We huddled together, sharing coats and wraps. Some began to sing :

"The sea, the sea, the open sea."

Others went below. The sea was too open for them. I peered down a hatchway where tea was being brewed in a black pot. No, it was preferable to stay on deck.

Crowlin Island loomed ahead. As we passed we could see the thatched cottages and a few stray animals.

The island had once supported a population of thirty, but now only a few elderly people remained. There was nothing there to satisfy youth, no recreation, no amusement, merely the possibility of bare existence.

As for the aged, there were no roads, no proper footpaths even, on the island. There was no harbour, not even a small pier for motor-boats, and the only access to the shore was by a precipitous winding track. There was not even a post-office where the aged could draw their old-age pension !

Farther on we hove-to as a rowing-boat came alongside. One of our party whose home was at Toscaig was transferred to it and quickly rowed away. We passed several other boats, their occupants being busily engaged fishing. The " lines " were invariably cast on the right side of the boat. I asked why.

" It says that in the Book," I was told. For the Bible is a guide to the fisherman in his hazardous occupation.

The sea was calm as we sailed into Applecross Bay and tied up at the little pier at Milton. Although the hour was late, no one seemed to have gone to bed. The people must have been in agreement with Dr. Johnson's remark, " Whoever thinks of going to bed before midnight is a scoundrel." They were all honest folks in Applecross.

The village consisted of a row of small, trim houses. The Inn, or Temperance Hotel as it is now called, was owned by Mrs. Macrae, an elderly lady of very fine character. I had met her on several occasions and had a great regard for her. She had one weakness ; she gave so freely to Foreign Mission funds that, when in ripeness of years she died, she was without means.

Passing through the village, we crossed the river to

the church which stands, surrounded by the churchyard, on the other side of the bay. Beside the old church stood the Manse. It was very late when we got there but, as I should be leaving early in the morning, Mr. Laing and I decided to have a look round.

Picture us, therefore, at midnight in that old churchyard, exploring historic tombstones and prehistoric stones and deciphering ancient inscriptions by the feeble light of matches. Imagine the feelings of anyone passing by, seeing the flickering flame at that untimely hour !

We stood on the spot where Saint Maelrubha had founded his monastery ; around us stretched sacred territory or sanctuary. The Saint had founded many other churches both in Skye and on the Mainland. In all of these he had preached frequently.

Despite the non-existence of train, aeroplane, or car, he had travelled widely. In this respect, at least, it may be said that the Highland ministers of to-day are faithfully following his example.

During a visit to Urquhart in Ross, Saint Maelrubha was fatally wounded by Norwegians who landed on the coast there. Realising he was dying, he asked to be taken back to Applecross where he desired to be buried. He was carried home and died a few days later, on 21st April, 722, at the age of eighty years, three months and nineteen days.

We returned to the Manse where a welcome supper awaited us. I did ample justice to it and soon retired to rest, but not to sleep. The bed was comfortable, but the house was old. The church had been erected in 1817, and I had felt it would have been discourteous to have enquired about the age of the house. It seemed that,

" O'er all there hung a shadow and a fear ;
    A sense of mystery and spirit daunted,
   And said as plain as whisper to the ear,
     The place is haunted."

Next morning I was up before sunrise, and after a
hurried breakfast, set out for the pier accompanied by
Mr. Laing. On that lovely morning I could appreciate
the beauty of the scene. Certainly Saint Maelrubha had
chosen a delightful setting for his monastery.

It is regrettable that a like love of the beautiful did
not permeate our nineteenth century Christians. The old
church differed in appearance from a barn only by the
Cross on the east gable ; and even that, Mr. Laing told me,
was found buried under the church floor. During recent
renovations of the church, it had been found and restored
to its original position.

We crossed the substantial bridge which spans the river.
To the left, surrounded by trees, stands Applecross House,
the residence of the laird of Applecross who was at that time
Lord Middleton. The present owner is Captain Wills.

A tree which marks the heart of the Sanctuary was
pointed out to me. In olden days, any criminal sheltering
within six miles of this spot was immune from arrest. But
times had changed. There was even a village policeman,
although I understand there was so little crime that he was
allowed to carry on the trade of a plumber !

The village was then, and still is, mainly dependent
on the steamboat service for passenger and freight transport. True, according to the map, Applecross is actually
on the Scottish mainland. Theoretically, a road connects
it with Lochcarron, nineteen miles distant ; but in
practice, the connection only applies when there are no
snowstorms or landslides.

The road is one of the wonders of Scotland. It has been engineered as a series of zig-zags to ease the gradients, some of which are one in seven. Rising from sea-level at Applecross, it reaches the summit six miles farther on at a height of over two thousand feet, again descending to sea-level by an even more freakish series of bends and curves and twistings.

The motorist who ventures up this road will be amply rewarded by the magnificent view, but the driver will have no time for scenery. At one moment he will be facing the the east ; the next, he will be looking towards the west ; in a brief period he will have turned in every direction. An ideal road for a politician !

I chose the straight road south by steamboat. The arrival of the *Shiela* was now about due, so I said good-bye to my host and hurried along to the pier which I reached as the ship hove in sight.

A number of people had gathered. Mrs. Macrae, The Inn, was there, also Mrs. MacDonald whom I knew, and several others. One, in particular, was the missionary.

It may seem strange to mention the presence of a missionary at this time in such an early outpost of Christianity. But a missionary, in the Highlands, simply means a lay reader or a preacher who has not had the full theological training, and one who accordingly receives a smaller salary than a minister. Incidentally, the monetary reward which a minister receives is called a stipend.

That morning the midges were out in full force. It may be that it is their custom to rise at five o'clock in the morning. Certainly it is not mine ; and if the viciousness displayed by them that morning was a result, it was an example not to be lightly followed.

The missionary held a peculiar attraction for them. He was dressed in faded black—for, to preach the Gospel, one must go into mourning—and they literally covered him. His hat was grey, alive with them.

The *Shiela* drew near; a rowing-boat was ready to pull out. Good-byes had to be said. Mrs. Macrae kissed each one as they left. No, she did not kiss the missionary, but I saw her coming towards me.

I was young, then. In desperation I turned to Mrs. MacDonald.

" Will she kiss me, too ? " I asked.

Mrs. MacDonald was most unsympathetic, most unhelpful. I saw no cause for levity. Mrs. Macrae drew near . . .

13

DISTINGUISHED VISITORS

LORD BLYTHSWOOD was one of the first visitors whom I remember. He had leased Balmacara House for a term of years, and he resided there during a part of each year. He was a man of very strong character. Born in different surroundings, he would have been a Free Presbyterian. As it happened, he was a clergyman of the Church of England.

He sometimes preached in our church in Kyle. A tall, well-built man, garbed in a long, much-worn cassock, he presented a typically Presbyterian appearance. The last time he took the service was the occasion of the dedication of a Communion Table which he had presented to the church.

The Table was a replica of one in All Saints' Church, Derby, of which he, the Reverend Sholto Douglas, had been Vicar. In lieu of a sermon, he entertained us with the story of his battle there. When he had become Vicar of All Saints he had found what he called a " stone altar " in the church. An old oak table had been relegated to a minor position where it was used for resting coffins. Upon enquiry, he had found that the oak table was the original Holy Table.

" I cast out the stone altar," thundered his lordship, and his Presbyterian congregation were tempted to applaud—they may have added, " Amen,"—" And I put the Holy Table back in its rightful place."

His churchwardens had objected to the change. The matter had been fought out in the church courts where the Vicar had won. They had appealed to the House of Lords. Again he had won. Having won, he had paid all costs. That was typical of him.

He had a large yacht, the *Sgian Dhu*, in which he cruised among the lochs. On one occasion he had been shopping at Kyle, and, half-way back to Balmacara, unexpectedly gave orders to return. He had discovered that a merchant had given him incorrect change. The big yacht was turned and brought back immediately. His lordship got his missing fourpence and was satisfied. What did it matter about the cost of a few extra tons of coal ?

During Lord Blythswood's residence at Balmacara, the estate changed ownership, and the new proprietor sold many of the trees. The purchaser set up a sawmill on the avenue leading to Balmacara House. Lord Blythswood, as tenant, objected. He went to law. The case was fought out in the Court of Session where he won. The sequel was what might have been anticipated. He allowed the sawmill to remain.

The next peer of the realm whom I encountered was Lord Knutsford. I met him first before he succeeded to the title, when he was spending a holiday in Skye. Later, he went regularly to the Outer Isles to fish and shoot. He often spent a few days at Kyle when going or returning.

He told me that he wrote regularly to his ghillies in Scotland whom he regarded not merely as servants but as personal friends. I remember one evening, after dinner, he related some of his experiences in connection with the London hospitals. He was remarking upon the number of Scots doctors there. He said he had a high regard for them, they were all such fine fellows.

" The fact is," he went on, " Every Scotsman is a born gentleman." He paused, looked across to me, then added quizzically, " Present company excepted ! "

One morning a friend of mine, Dr. Isaac MacIver of Fort William, arrived at Kyle by the early boat from Stornoway. Not wishing to disturb us at five o'clock in the morning, he went to the Station Hotel for breakfast. Glancing at the Visitors' Book, he found that the last entry had been written right across the page. The name stood out boldly :

" The Viscount Knutsford."

Now Dr. MacIver, a native of Shawbost, a small crofting township in Lewis, held only such distinctions as he had won by hard work. He had not inherited them. He had served as an officer in the Great War and was now a brilliant member of his profession. But he was an ardent socialist. And here, before him, was flaunted a hereditary title.

He saw red. He took up a pen, and in equally glaring caligraphy, wrote :

" The Earl of Shawbost."

Perhaps one of our most regular visitors for many years was the Right Reverend Bishop Lang, D.D. During his annual holiday Dr. Lang might have been seen any day cycling along the roadway, or on foot by loch and moor, out in all states of the weather, warm or cold, in sunshine or rain, drinking in the beauty of the scenes he knows so well.

It is not only as an English bishop and the brother of an archbishop that we like to think of Dr. Lang. We revere him as the son of a great Scotsman, the late Very Reverend Dr. Marshall Lang, Principal of Aberdeen University. In appearance the bishop is tall, wiry, and distinguished-looking. Even in non-clerical garb and wheeling an old black enamelled bicycle, he presents a striking figure.

Perhaps he hardly conforms to our Presbyterian ideas of a clergyman ; at least not to those of my daughter Mary. One evening she was returning by train from Plockton, where she attended school. Along with other pupils, it seems she had entered the compartment where the bishop was seated. One of the girls had tripped over his long legs, with the result that his lordship may have uttered an involuntary " Damn," surely excusable in the circumstances.

But Mary holds very strict views. When I met her at the station, her first words were :

" Daddy, surely he can't be a bishop. He swore at us."

I cannot mention the bishop without being reminded of Mr. and Mrs. Gordon who, until quite recently, were annual visitors about the same time. Mr. Gordon was

H

lecturer at Cambridge and, during the month he spen with us each year, his brown crotal suit, as he walke through the village, proclaimed to all that August wa with us again.

A few years ago, when touring in Skye, Mr. Gordo came upon a ditched car, one in which an inexperience woman driver had vainly attempted to pass anothe vehicle. The road was only wide enough for one car, bu this poor female had no head for mathematics.

Unfortunately for Mr. Gordon, he was one of thos who went to her assistance. Now anyone who has take part in a tug-of-war knows that there are two ways o pulling. One is to pull with all your might. The other i to put your hands on the rope, puff out your cheeks an look as if you were doing it all, but leaving the real pullin to the others.

So it was with this lady's car. Some shouted an fussed, but Mr. Gordon was one of those who did the actua pulling. He received a severe strain, from the effects o which he never fully recovered.

It seems that I have not yet finished with members o the peerage. Lord Leverhulme is the next whom I recal He dressed in a distinctive manner, possibly in order no to be mistaken for his butler. He wore a light gre morning coat of special cut. His hat, also light grey, wa of a shape once much favoured by Scottish farmers and I believe, sometimes called the " Daily Mail " hat.

His lordship was very deaf, a fact of which I wa unaware until too late. I had made a commonplac remark about the weather, mentioning something whicl no doubt he already knew ; yet he insisted on my repeatin it. So there I stood, shouting as loudly as I could, tha the day was warm. And I felt it, too !

Lord Leverhulme was not content to follow in a rut. Because our grandfathers when travelling to Stornoway had made the journey wholly by sea, he did not consider this a sufficient reason for doing the same. The normal sea-crossing, a distance of sixty-two miles, occupied four or five hours. His lordship decided that this meant waste of time.

He studied the map, planned his route, and acted accordingly. Arriving at Kyle of Lochalsh, he crossed the ferry to Kyleakin ; thence he went by car to Dunvegan, crossed by boat to Harris and continued north by car to Stornoway. The Minch had now become a mere ferry.

But Lord Leverhulme had not counted the cost. He had altered the established order of things ; and, unforgivable offence, he had relegated Stornoway to a minor position on the Isle of Lewis and Harris.

I have entered the names of the foregoing visitors, as far as practicable, in the order in which I met them. That is the reason why I record the visit of Their Majesties at this stage. I should state that the sense in which I met them was that I stood with a camera as they passed by.

Their Royal Highnesses the Duke and Duchess of York arrived at Kyle of Lochalsh on 11th September, 1933. The waiting crowd gave them an enthusiastic welcome as the train steamed in. I stood alongside pressmen and photographers. Just as the engine stopped, a grey cat crossed the rails and jumped on to the platform.

" There is the incident we want," said one of the pressmen, " A cat for luck."

" It ought to be a black cat," I pointed out.

" It will be a black cat by the time my story appears tomorrow," he replied, with conviction. Evidently an

apt disciple of the newspaper lord who never bothered
about inconvenient facts !

The Duke and Duchess walked along the pier, followed
by the notabilities of the district. They were piped on
board a motor launch which carried them to the Yacht,
Golden Hind, owned by Commander Kitson, R.N., and
anchored in the bay. They spent some time on the yacht,
so I crossed the ferry to Kyleakin and was waiting on the
pier when they landed there.

A policeman mentioned, almost casually, that I ought
not to be there without a permit. But he did not know
that my grandmother was a MacCrimmon ! What clan
had a better right to be represented when guests of The
MacLeod arrived ?   A permit for a MacCrimmon to set
foot on Skye ! Shades of Sir Walter Scott, it was enough
to make him rise and write a fresh lament !

Most people write books to-day, so this must be my
excuse for now mentioning the names of several authors.
Those who have read H. V. Morton's fascinating book,
In Search of Scotland, may remember that Mr. Morton,
arriving in Kyle on a Saturday, had an experience with
the local chemist on the following day. It would seem,
therefore, that I have met Mr. Morton. Hoots,
mon !

Another author about whom I have a more vivid
recollection is D. K. Broster, whose books, particularly her
Jacobite ones, are exceedingly popular. Miss Broster had
been spending a holiday at Kinlochewe and, at the request
of a mutual acquaintance, called on me when she visited
Kyle. I found her as charming as her books.

Shortly after her visit I met C. J. Cutcliffe Hyne, the
famous author of *Captain Kettle*. Mr. Hyne told me that
he had resided on the West Coast for a number of years and

ROYAL LANDING IN SKYE

had a great love for it.   He had just given an interview to
a pressman regarding the state of the Highlands.

After he returned home he wrote me.   He said that
the Scottish papers had given it to him in the neck, and
that they couldn't have been more uncivil if he had been a
politician instead of a private citizen trying to buck up a
part of the country he was proud of.

I have since read Mr. Hyne's most interesting book,
West Highland Spirits, and I must admit he is a bit hard
on our easy-going ways.

Two local authors may be mentioned.   One is Cynthia
Fraser, gifted author of *Quest*.   Perhaps I ought not to
include Miss Fraser in a list of visitors, for she makes her
home in Lochalsh for part of the year.   She is the daughter
of the late Sir Hugh Fraser, proprietor of Stromeferry,
judge of the High Court, and himself a noted author.   Miss
Fraser has built for herself a residence on the shore of
Lochalsh.   It is a modern house with a thatched roof and
is called by a Gaelic name meaning, " The Harbour of
Peace."

The other is Margaret Leigh whose first book,
Highland Homespun, raised a hornet's nest in the district.
She, too, built a home for herself which she occupied for
several years.   She also rented and worked a farm.   In
her spare time she rode on horseback through the parish
collecting material for the masterpiece which she later
produced.

It is said that a semi-retired statesman of Celtic blood
would begin a speech in the most moderate and friendly
manner possible, then, warming to his subject, he would
throw tact to the winds.   He would roll fine phrases round
his tongue, breathing fire and brimstone.

So it may have been with Miss Leigh in her description

of some of our local characters. Gifted as an English scholar, her very gift of words may have led her in some instances to paint a picture, admirable as literature but not always appreciated by the unfortunate victims !

Another author whom, chronologically, I might have mentioned at an earlier period, is the Reverend J. M. McPherson, D.D., author of *Primitive Beliefs in the North East of Scotland*. Having known Dr. McPherson all my life, I am always pleased when he visits us.

It may have been due to his particular brand of humour—I have been told that it runs in the family—that he once told me he had seen some sign of civilisation in Kyle at last. The " sign " was a pot-hole. Since that time we must have become very highly civilised indeed.

One story which Dr. McPherson loves to tell concerns a husband and wife who had quarrelled. In such a case the parish minister was usually the arbiter. The wife went first to him with her tale.

" I told my man," she said, " that I would go to the minister," and he said, " You can go to the devil if you like ! "

A short time later the husband arrived at the Manse with his version of the quarrel, and this is how he began :

" My wife said she would go to the minister, so I said to her, ' The very man.' "

Synonymous !

Dr. D. J. MacLeod, formerly H.M. Inspector of Schools in the North of Scotland, has visited us regularly for many years. One of our most distinguished Highlanders, Dr. MacLeod is a brilliant linguist. Even in our small community he occasionally finds opportunity to exercise his talent.

At one moment speaking in English, the next in

Gaelic, he will converse with my neighbour, Mr. Harris Gordon, in his native tongue. I have witnessed the keen delight of the old exile as he listened to the once familiar words of his beloved Poland.

Dr. MacLeod has the gift of quiet humour. He relates an incident which occurred at Kyle. Calum, the hotel boots, had returned from the harbour.

" Did any passengers come off the boat ? " he was asked.

" Yes," said Calum, " there were three."

" Who were they ? " persisted his questioner.

Calum answered in all seriousness,

" A gentleman, a commercial traveller, and a man from Skye."

Sheriff Trotter, K.C., likes to visit Skye, and he is another we love to see. He recently wrote a legal book, so learned that there is no critic with sufficient knowledge to criticise it !

He once remarked that the use of big words held a singular attraction for some people, particularly those who did not understand them. On one occasion, when staying at a Highland hotel, he was about to ascend the stairs when a maid passed him hurriedly, with the apology,

" Allow me to predecease you, sir."

" With the greatest of pleasure," replied the sheriff instantly and, no doubt, sincerely.

Each summer brings new faces. Many visitors come again and again ; and it is a pleasure to welcome them as the years go by. Others are merely ships that pass.

Seldom a year passes but I meet visitors from Canada or the United States who have come to see the old land of which they have heard so often from parents or grandparents. Many Englishmen, too, coming north for a holiday, are happy to remember that they have a Highland ancestor.

For a number of years Sir Kenneth Murchison, a former Mayor of Hertford and M.P. for East Hull, has been a frequent visitor. He is a descendant of Colonel Murchison, whose monument—erected in 1863 by his great-grand-nephew, Sir Roderick Murchison, the distinguished geologist—still stands out, a prominent landmark on the shores of Lochalsh.

The monument was damaged by lightning in 1927. Sir Kenneth was, at the time, in attendance at the House of Commons where he received the following surprising telegram from a clansman in Kyle :

"Murchison Monument struck by lighting.   Wire instructions!"

Here was a poser for the honourable member for East Hull !   He told me he was tempted to reply, " Don't let it occur again," but he feared that this would have been considered too flippant for his pious kinsmen.   Curiously enough, it did occur again—the monument being struck a second time several months later, when it was found to be so badly damaged that it had to be completely rebuilt.

I shall close this chapter with the name of one more visitor, that of Mr. G. F. Mowatt, one of the most charming persons I have been privileged to meet.   I was introduced to him at his special request.   He was a finely built man of striking appearance.

He greeted me with a warm, friendly smile.   His voice was pleasant and gentle.   He held out his hand, gropingly.   Only then did I realise he was blind.   Oh, the pity !

Although his eyes are sightless, Mr. Mowatt can sense the beauty of mountain and loch, the wonder of sunrise and sunset. He loves yachting and boating. He is proud to enjoy the friendship of the Duke of Windsor whom he has known for many years.

He related an incident which occurred at a banquet where the Duke, then the Prince of Wales, presided, and at which he was one of the guests.

As usual the whole company rose when the Prince entered, and remained standing until he was seated. Later, when the meat course was brought in, all rose again. The Prince had got up to perform a service, and the whole company remained standing. Mr. Mowatt also rose although he did not know the reason. He was to learn later. It was yet another instance of the Prince's warm humanity.

After the banquet Mr. Mowatt asked for his waiter, in order to thank him for cutting his meat into small pieces, a necessity owing to his blindness. The waiter replied,

" I did not cut the meat for you, sir. His Royal Highness did that."

14

GLOMACH

THE Public Holidays which the Kyle Council had fixed for its inhabitants had one drawback. What was the use of a holiday if one had to stay at home ? To the young, at anyrate, a holiday suggests an outing, a trip somewhere. But where could we in Kyle go, with the hope of returning the same day ?

A journey to Inverness, in order to spend even a few hours there, would involve seven or eight hours' rail travel. Not exactly a pleasure jaunt !

On this first June holiday a number of us decided to visit the Fall of Glomach. The highest waterfall in Great Britain, one of the marvels of our Western Highlands, none of our party had yet seen it. Information about it was strangely meagre. We consulted several popular Scottish guide books, only to find no mention of it.

An encyclopædia published by a great newspaper firm whose slogan was, " Buy British," was next consulted. This work was found to contain several illustrations of a smaller American fall, but the British one was entirely ignored. At length we obtained particulars through the courtesy of the librarian of Aberdeen Public Library.

Unlike Niagara which is composed of several small falls, the highest being only 182 feet, Glomach is, when in flood, one complete fall 370 feet in height.

We learnt from an Ordnance map that it lay twenty-two miles due east of Kyle, and that a road passed within two miles of it. There was no motor-omnibus in the district, and cars were few. The state of the roads did not encourage cycling.

There was, however, a motor-lorry, a vehicle sometimes used at funerals, the coffin occupying the centre, with planks placed along the sides to seat the mourners. We resolved to travel by this conveyance ; so, picture us on that bright summer morning setting out for Glomach, equipped with lunch baskets and cameras.

The first ten miles were covered in less than an hour. Quick travel ! We turned off the main road at Ardelve, and proceeded even more slowly along the side of Loch Long.

Not even the jolting of the motor-lorry on that narrow winding road, or the ever-increasing hardness of the seats, could spoil our enjoyment. Below us stretched Loch Long, dark and beautiful. Across its waters rose the pine-clad mountain ridges. The sun beat down hotly from a cloudless sky.

The county road terminates at Killilan. Beyond this the private road—which has been built along an old right-of-way—was in much better condition. We journeyed leisurely along until we reached Carnoch Loch.

A quick tramp over the moor and down to the loch soon restored the circulation to our aching limbs. We crossed by stepping-stones at the end of the loch, then kept straight on to the River Glomach, only a short distance beyond. Following a spell of dry weather, we found the river unusually low and not difficult to cross.

Our route lay up the south side of the river. The track, where discernible, followed the bank of the stream, then ascended steeply, winding tortuously round the hillside and again dipping down. We crossed a tributary near its confluence with the river, then climbed up the green hillside to a point where the path cuts under an overhanging ledge.

Here we had the first glimpse of the top of the fall, half a mile distant. We heard the roar of the waters thundering down to the abyss. We followed the dizzy track, keeping well up from the bed of the river. High up on the hillside we joined the path from Dorisduan.

Immediately below there was a green ledge surmounted by a tree, which projected over the chasm, opposite the fall. We descended to this spot, so considerately provided by Nature in order that we might view one of her mighty marvels.

I had brought with me a panorama camera, one with a moving lens capable of photographing anything visible. Unlike the present-day luxury cameras, it was bulky, awkwardly shaped, and difficult to handle.

I lay outstretched upon the grass, with this unwieldy instrument held as far as possible over the gorge. Two companions seated themselves firmly on my legs. To add to my discomfort, I was assailed by a horde of midges which, apparently realising my helpless position, attacked me with hitlerish cunning.

Without a periscope it was impossible to see to the foot of the abyss, so, hoping for the best, I pressed the trigger release. The result was a photograph showing the whole 370 feet of the fall. In a sense, as I was to learn later, this was a prehistoric photograph !

Ten years after this visit, a great national daily newspaper gave to the world its discovery of the Fall of Glomach ! It appeared that two members of the newspaper's staff had succeeded at great peril in photographing it for the first time !

While it is true that Glomach is more than twice the height of the highest of the Niagara Falls, it must be conceded that the American Fall has a greater volume of water. I had visited Glomach after a spell of fine weather when the river was abnormally low. I resolved at the first opportunity to see it after a period of rain.

About this time I became the owner of a motor-cycle. It was called the " Mackenzie," and had a band of the tartan of that great clan enamelled on the tank. The registration number was JS 1715. A keen Jacobite, I hailed this reminder of the date of James Stuart's bid for his throne as a happy omen.

I ought to have remembered that the 1715 rising,

even with the assistance of the Mackenzies of Kintail, was a miserable failure ; and the Mackenzie motor cycle was not wholly a success. In theory, the engine could be assisted by pedalling. In practice, I found that the human leg was incapable of attaining and maintaining the speed required.

One morning, after two days of a steady downpour, the rain suddenly ceased and the sun came out. Judging this to be a suitable time for seeing Glomach at its best I mounted my steed and, after some initial hesitation on the part of the engine, set out for the Fall.

I reached Killilan in record time, and, to my own astonishment, without mishap. Mr. Melville Wills, proprietor of Killilan, granted me permission to proceed along his private road—for the road beyond Killilan Lodge, although it follows an old right-of-way, belongs to Mr. Wills in the sense that he bears the cost of upkeep.

Mr. Wills told me that the river was too swollen to cross, and advised me to approach the fall from the high ground above Carnoch. Accordingly I kept straight on along the lochside to the house at the head of Carnoch, occupied by Kenneth Finlayson.

" Good rarely comes from good advice," wrote Byron, who probably had bitter experience. And the good advice I received from Mr. Wills was to land me on the dizzy brink of a precipice !

I found Mr. Finlayson at home, and he insisted on accompanying me as guide. We set out up the glen, following a zig-zag pony track which wound up the mountainside. We crossed the moor at a speed which suggested the presence of a distillery at the other end.

My guide marched on ahead of me, his long legs swinging across the moor, mile after mile at the same relentless pace. I was almost exhausted when at last we came in sight of the River Glomach as it curved like a silver ribbon across the plateau above the fall.

We now left the path, clambering over moss-covered boulders and down the almost perpendicular hillside. We halted at a narrow crevice within a stone's throw of the fall.

I attempted to get some photographs, but without much success. There was no room to move. To bend forward—and continue this earthly existence—was an impossibility.

Beneath was a sheer drop of some four hundred feet. All around was grey barren rock. The hills seemed to be closing in. The noise of the waters became torture. . . . I packed up my camera.

" Let us get back," I cried.

Away Finlayson went, again at full speed. Up that hillside he climbed as if Satan and all his satellites were pursuing him. Once he paused to look back.

" Don't put your foot on there," he counselled, indicating a bank of peat which he had partially dislodged. Well-meant advice, but there was nowhere else to tread. The only course was to step on it and beyond, before the slow-moving turf could plunge down to the depths.

It was with a sigh of relief that I reached the top. But my guide had no time to meditate upon our deliverance from peril; he was off again, speeding back across the moor.

Without further incident, and in what I feel must have been record time, we reached Carnoch House where Mrs. Finlayson had tea prepared for us. And as we sat enjoying the fragrant cup, Mr. Finlayson casually remarked,

" I was never that way before ! "

Following this experience I visited Glomach on several occasions during dry spells whenever opportunity occurred. I still hankered after a sight of the fall in full flood. It is the unattainable which appeals.

One day I was talking to Dr. Macrae, and mentioned my difficulty in crossing the river when in spate. Dr. Macrae is our parish doctor. He has an extensive practice, covering an area of a thousand square miles. Although much of his travel is done by car, he also uses a motor-cycle. There are also remote homesteads accessible only on foot.

He has to cross ferries by boat. He has to walk over the rough moorland or along desolate glens. He spoke of one house which seemed to be needlessly difficult of access. It was so near and yet so far.

The roadway lay along the opposite side of the river from the house, but for some obscure reason the bridge crossing to it was a mile lower down. Now the doctor's time was precious. He solved his difficulty by stopping his car opposite the house; he then donned a pair of fishermen's waders and walked across the river bed.

Here was inspiration ! I would visit Glomach when the river was in flood, and I would walk through the waters. So I purchased a pair of waders.

Many people who visit the west coast of Scotland in summer go away with the impression that the climate is not so dry as it might be. Dry ! Had they visited Kyle that summer, they would have had their heart's desire of drought.

All that June the sun shone down pitilessly. The ground became parched. The grass withered and died. No cloud appeared in the sky. The beauty of mountain and loch departed.

In July there was little improvement. True, there were cold east winds and threatening clouds when holiday-makers appeared during the Glasgow Fair week. But still no rain fell, and the Glomach river dropped lower and lower.

But waders have various uses. It happens that, running through my garden, there is a small stream, its source a deep spring which never dries up. At the point where the stream enters through the boundary fence, there was a marshy corner of unfathomed depths. Here in the slime an eel would be occasionally seen uncoiling itself and rearing up its ugly head. I detested the creatures immensely.

So I put on my waders, got a pick, a spade, a shovel, a rake and every other tool which my garden possessed, and I set to work. It was hard work, hot work, dirty work ; but I routed these reptiles and I cleared the bed of the stream.

And then the rain came. It rained night and day for a fortnight, good, honest, wet rain. There was no trickery, no uncertainty about the matter. No-one was misled into going out without a raincoat or umbrella. The rain poured down steadily, continuously, relentlessly.

Then one morning it stopped. Oh, the glory of that August morning !

About this time Mr. John MacDonald, police-sergeant at Kyle, got a motor-cycle and side-car. It was his first motor-cycle, and anyone who has had a similar experience will understand how he felt.

Crime ! There was no crime in Lochalsh. Every dog had a collar, and every sheep had been dipped. Hang regulations, he would take a day off.

So he asked me to accompany him to Glomach. It

was an ideal day for the purpose. The waders were to be tested at last. We even fixed up a complicated system of cords to act as a miniature blondin to take them dry across the river ; the idea being that I should cross first, then remove the waders which Mr. MacDonald would pull back for his own use. The difference in the size of feet was one of several factors we overlooked.

Perhaps Mr. MacDonald was not a very expert driver, but I always find a smooth run, whether on land or sea, a bit monotonous. This trip was not. I held on grimly to the side-car as we bounded over a boulder or swung sharply round a blind corner.

All went well until we reached Sallachy, a crofting township near the head of Loch Long. A level piece of road stretched straight ahead. Here was a chance to put on speed. A cow, grazing by the roadside, held other views.

Around the neck of this cow was a rope, the other end of which was fixed to a pin in the ground. The animal was tethered. She had wandered across the roadway, dragging the rope loosely behind. Mr. MacDonald decided to risk passing.

Alas, just at the instant he was about to pass, that wretched cow sprinted away, drawing the rope tightly across the roadway. With a grinding of gears we came to a sudden stop. It was our first check in a day of trial.

We could find no damage apparent. But clearly the cow ought not to have been tethered so near the roadway. It was a breach of the Highways Act. Here was crime at last !

But Mr. MacDonald was not in uniform. If he reported the offence it might be difficult to explain his presence there at a time when, theoretically, he was on

I

duty at Kyle. Life is just like that. The bovine cause of his dilemma flicked its tail and took another bite. We moved on.

Our next halt was at Killilan Lodge. Mr. Wills was interested in our trip, readily granting us permission to proceed along his road. He advised us to cross by a private foot-bridge which spans the river a few miles below Carnoch loch. He smiled at our mention of the waders, for Mr. Wills was an experienced fisherman and knew the river in all its moods. Heedless of advice, we kept recklessly on.

We halted above the loch, parking our vehicle at a recess in the roadway. Reaching the lochside, we found the stepping-stones hidden beneath the brown surging waters. Somewhat doubtfully I now tried on the waders, but it seemed that a diving suit would have been more appropriate in the circumstances. I stepped timidly in.

There was an unusual buoyancy about my feet. They seemed to have shrunk. They were becoming cold, and—horrible realisation—wet. Yes, the water was flowing in. It was penetrating cuts in the waders where the garden spade had done its fell work.

Reluctantly we turned back, resolved to take Mr. Wills' advice after all. Reaching the foot-bridge, we again parked our vehicle, then crossed the river. We now began a four miles' scramble up the south bank of the Glomach river.

Shall I ever forget that experience? Every fifty yards or so, a small stream or larger torrent, tributaries of the main river, had to be crossed. The whole mountain-side was gushing forth water for our torment.

At first we attempted to keep our feet dry by jumping

from boulder to boulder, but as we proceeded the streams increased in size and frequency. We became regardless of wetting and simply marched through the waters. Mile after mile we covered until at length we reached, high up on the hillside, the spot from which a first view of the fall is obtained.

There was no time—even if we had had sufficient vitality left—to make a closer approach and return before dusk. In the distance we could see the top of the white foaming fall as it leapt into space. We heard the thunder of the waters echoing and re-echoing among the grim desolate mountains.

We turned our backs and resumed our march through spate and flood. Tired and sodden we reached the foot-bridge. Wearily we limped across it. Our vehicle stood waiting and we were soon seated.

Mr. MacDonald attempted to start the engine, but for a time his efforts were in vain. At last he managed to coax it to make a feeble start and we proceeded homeward slowly. Stops were frequent, and we reached Killilan after dark. There the engine finally and definitely refused to function.

Abandoning the now useless cycle and side-car, we set out in the darkness on foot. Sixteen long miles lay ahead. We had had no meal since breakfast, and we were nearly exhausted. We were passing Sallachy when we noticed a shop with a garage alongside. What, a car for hire in this wilderness ? We knocked at the house door. Yes, there was a car. We were saved !

The ancient model of America's great invention was taken gently from its garage. Carbide lamps were brought out and then very slowly and deliberately filled and lighted. The ignition had to be tested, the oil tank examined. Various adjustments had to be made. For this was an occasion!

As we tramped about, trying to keep warm and impatient to be gone, there came to our ears the joyous lowing of a cow in a nearby shed. I verily believe she was the self-same animal we had encountered in the morning. And now she was rejoicing in the damage she had done, which had brought to her owner the reward of a car hire.

Drinking whisky and eating Scotch broth are two habits which can only be acquired by dogged perseverance. No normal person really cares for the vile taste of either.

Glomach, too, is an acquired taste. I found that each successive visit had been merely a fresh occasion for further trial and misfortune. Nevertheless I persisted, and a summer seldom passed without at least one trip.

Perhaps one of my most interesting outings was a recent one in company with a party of young women. My companions were modern members of their sex. Dressed in bathing costumes, one hot summer day, they took me by car to the lochside. The river crossing was literally a walk-over.

Giddy heights and yawning chasms held no terrors for them. They were impervious to the attacks of midges and mosquitoes. These insects found on my wretched limbs all the sustenance they needed.

For in a moment of weakness I had shed the greater part of my normal covering, and my long legs were now encased in a pair of khaki shorts several sizes too small. The American trippers whom we met might have been pardoned for mistaking me for George Bernard Shaw just returned from the Riviera!

In these days when cars are plentiful and reliable,

ON THE GLOMACH RIVER

and when roads are slightly improved, it is certainly less difficult to reach the lochside. Beyond that there is no change.

No generous landowner has seen fit to span the river with a foot-bridge, or to fix up guide-posts along the path.

No, the plain truth must be told. The landowners do not want sightseers. They want peace. They are in the wrong world !

15

VILLAGE HALLS

THERE is such a scarcity of public halls in many towns that, at the time of a General Election, the party which books the largest one—it may be the only one—is regarded as the best tactician. Kyle, in its short history, has had quite a number of halls.

The first one to be built was called the Kyle Institute. The name appears to have been given by a liberal donor to the fund for its use and upkeep. It is strange how worthy people so often temper their good deeds. Institute ! The very name savours of a home for lepers.

The building was roofed with corrugated iron, and ornamented at each gable with an iron cross. It was intended to be used for religious services and social gatherings, and a condition was embodied in its constitution that not more than two dances might be held in any one year.

Oh yes, the good people permitted, no doubt with much inward misgiving, the holding of two dances per annum. But—twice naughty only; for they had no doubt but that much dancing would lead to perdition!

The Young Women's Guild held their meetings there. And very happy gatherings they sometimes were. After tea, and perhaps a little gossip, these girls, their ages ranging from sixteen to sixty, would enjoy a game of musical chairs, in which even the missionary might participate. Oh, the thrill!

There were winter evenings when the doctor held his ambulance class. He was young and unmarried. The young women developed a keenness for ambulance work and attended in record numbers. So the young men went to guide them home, and Alick Munro proved to be one of the most popular and interesting guides.

Mr. Munro is now a railway guard, and one of our highly esteemed townsmen. He is, in fact, such a near neighbour of my own, that I can lie in bed listening to his poultry announcing the arrival of a fresh supply of eggs. I am indeed thankful that he does not also produce the raw material for bacon.

But in the early days of the Institute, Mr. Munro had not yet settled down. So it happened that he arrived late at the ambulance meeting one evening. He appeared to be drowsy. The doctor continued with his lecture for a time, then, thinking that Alick was not attending, he pounced on him with a question.

"What would you do if you found a man lying unconscious at the roadside, with his leg broken?" he asked.

Probably Alick did not have the foggiest idea, but he had no intention of giving himself away. He looked his questioner innocently in the face, and replied,

"Indeed, doctor, I think I would have a look to see what was in his pockets."

The Drill Hall was the next to be built. It was erected by the Territorial Association, primarily for training purposes, but was also available for dances and concerts. The old Institute had become too small. This was not entirely due to an increase in population but partly to a changing outlook. A " friendly glass " was no longer the only pleasure which the clergy tolerated. Now one might even attend a whist drive without fear of eternal damnation.

The Drill Hall possessed no platform, no seating accommodation, no lighting system ; but in spite of these and other drawbacks many entertainments were held there. An account of a Jacobite concert, typical of others, may give an idea of the difficulties with which the organisers had to contend.

As I have mentioned in an earlier chapter, the Kyle Council had to raise money for its various activities by voluntary methods. The streets were lighted by carbide gas lamps, and a lamp-lighter had to be paid. With true Scots' frugality, the lamps were only lit in the absence of moonlight, thus reducing the cost by half.

It is true that the lamplighter's idea of when the moon was due to appear was often at variance with reality. I am inclined to believe that the almanac which he consulted was out of date.

On this occasion it was decided to hold a concert to augment the funds. A programme was mapped out, artistes interviewed, and rehearsals set agoing. A Jacobite play was to be the main item, and this required a considerable amount of preparation, not the least of which was the acquisition by loan, theft, or guile, of various ancient articles of ladies' attire.

Large posters announced the forthcoming concert.

Mr. John Stewart had consented to be chairman. We vainly tried to make him change his Christian name for the occasion, but he flatly refused to be called Charles. There are times when even the nicest people can be exceedingly stubborn.

The Isles were scoured for Highland dress, suitable for male artistes. Mr. George Adam, wireless operator on the Stornoway boat, came to our help with several kilts and military uniforms. Yet in our search for appropriate garb, we had not dreamt of going back to Adam.

An interesting publicity campaign was set in motion. The concert being in aid of the lighting fund, a local bard chose the occasion to outrival Tennyson with an up-to-date version of " The Charge of the Light Brigade."

The hall was got ready on the evening preceding the concert. A platform was erected and covered with a borrowed carpet. Curtains were fixed in position, to form stage and anterooms. The Scottish Standard was there without permission of the Lyon King-of-arms.

The piano was next brought up from the Institute, perched precariously on a railway barrow. It was unloaded at the door and wheeled half-way across the hall. As the workers paused for a moment, a bright youth, who had been standing with hands in pockets, now sauntered forward and, placing a chair in front, sat down and commenced to play.

It was probably the only tune he knew. I cannot say, as one tune is the same as another to me. But that simple youth little realised his peril, for never surely did he have a less appreciative audience. The workers simply wheeled away the piano, leaving the budding musical genius seated alone in the middle of the hall.

Next day Mr. Pollock was early astir with his familiar

black horse and box-cart. He collected chairs and
wooden forms from the Institute, more chairs from hotels,
shops, and private houses ; and he carted these, all free of
cost, to the hall.   He even brought seats from the waiting-
rooms at the railway station ; for these were the days of
the old Highland Railway when an application had not to
be sent to London.

The concert was a memorable one.   Every man wore
the tartan of his clan or of the House of Stuart.   Each
woman, too, wore skirt or kilt of her clan.   And oh, how
the rafters echoed to the skirl of the bagpipes, and how
each item was applauded.

When Miss MacRae recited, her clan cheered themselves hoarse as she told of " The Proud Chief of Kintail."
Miss Pollock sang delightfully ; even the staleness of the
news that Prince Charlie was now safe did not damp or
lessen the enthusiasm.

I do not recall the details of the play, but I remember
that Miss Montgomery retired to the " withdrawing-room,"
and that Mr. Middleton, an officer of the Prince's army, lay
mortally wounded.   So realistic was the death scene that
the audience were, naturally, unable to hear what the
dying warrior said.

The Drill Hall had been the headquarters of the
Ross-shire Mountain Battery.   When the Great War was
declared the men at once volunteered for active service.
Guns and rifles were transferred elsewhere, to be employed
in training fresh recruits.   The most ardent pacifist could
not have objected to these weapons which were incapable
of being used effectively against an enemy.

As the war months dragged on, soldiers on leave and
bound for Skye or the Outer Isles, were continually
passing through Kyle.   Transport services were abnormal.

The submarine menace necessitated daylight sailing, and the darkened railway trains ran as circumstances permitted.

Men on leave had frequently to stay overnight in the village where food and accommodation were scarce. So the Red Cross Society fitted up the Drill Hall as a Soldiers' Rest. Mrs. Mackinnon of Dunringell, Mrs. Macrae, Kingillie, and Mr. J. Hosack, J.P., rendered invaluable service in organising the work.

In addition to soldiers whose homes were in the Islands, there came others. There came many from overseas, visiting Scotland for the first and perhaps the last time. These lads, sons and grandsons of men and women who, in preceding generations, had been hounded from our shores, had enlisted on the outbreak of war.

Sir Walter Scott, that great Lowland patriot, in writing about the Highland clearances, had under-estimated the Highland character when he wrote :

" If the hour of need should come, the pibroch may sound through the deserted region, but the summons will remain unanswered."

The hour had struck ; and the answer had come speedily from Canada, the United States, New Zealand, Australia. These young men had turned the other cheek to the oppressors of their ancestors. And now, on their first leave from the firing line, they came to see the old homes of their people in Skye and the Western Isles.

They came to visit the land which the sporting tenant now occupied, to look perhaps on the green mound where once had stood the homestead of a happy family. To give the sportsmen their due, they were no longer pursuing defenceless animals ; instead, they were engaged on more equal terms with an enemy who could hit back.

When the soldiers passed through Kyle they were assured of a welcome ; and sometimes the Drill Hall, even in those dark days, echoed to the skirl of the bag-pipes, and the sound of dancing could be heard. For our young women were proud to dance with these men in their brief respite from the miseries of war.

A brass tablet, placed upon an inside wall of the hall, now bears the following inscription :

THIS BUILDING WAS USED AS A REST FOR SOLDIERS AND SAILORS FROM 19th APRIL, 1916, TO 30th APRIL, 1919, IN CONNECTION WITH THE ROSS AND CROMARTY BRANCH RED CROSS SOCIETY. DURING THAT PERIOD 9,821 MEN WERE PUT UP FOR THE NIGHT, AND 32,022 MEALS WERE SERVED.

An American base was established at Kyle in the later years of the war. Sectional buildings were erected to house the young men employed in unloading cargoes of supplies from overseas. The Stars and Stripes floated above their temporary home.

A priest from Dornie, eleven miles distant, came to conduct Sunday morning services in the Drill Hall. A religious service at eight in the morning ! We began to realise how terrible a thing was war ! Why, good Presbyterians, the salt of the earth, we had been content to have our " morning " service at mid-day.

Peace came at last. The young men who had only recently reached the age for enlistment, and who had therefore seen little active service, came back, conquering heroes. A pitifully small band of battered veterans returned.

I remember one, a kinsman who had fought as a lad

in the South African War. He had held a good post in South America when the Great War broke out. His country called ; Lord Lovat called. Rory threw up his job at once, crossed the Atlantic, and rejoined his old regiment, the Lovat Scouts.

After his demobilisation, I went to the railway station to meet him. I met an old man, wasted with malaria, grey-haired, shrivelled.

All over the land, people began erecting War Memorials. It was good for the granite trade. The Government placed orders for medals which were turned out by the million. Again, it helped business.

Numerous soulless officials were appointed to administer a pensions' scheme. Medical men, members of the noble profession, hide-bound by rules and regulations —the ever-present help of the ignorant—and full of out-of-date theories, " examined " each applicant. My kinsman had no wounds, no scars, so was awarded no pension. A grateful country was content to let Rory die —and many like him.

After the years of war, even the hitherto unchanging Highlands began to change. Those youths who had glimpsed the outside world were restless, dissatisfied. They wanted excitement, amusement, entertainment. A travelling cinema appeared in the village. Concerts and dances took place more frequently. The Drill Hall, in its turn, became too small for the needs of the district.

Mr. John Stewart came forward with a proposal to build a Public Hall, and this was enthusiastically agreed to. In his years of work in raising funds and securing grants and loans, he had the keen support of Mr. M. Macpherson, schoolmaster, Mr. M. Gillies, treasurer to the fund, and indeed the whole community.

Meantime the Boy Scout Association, who had become owners of one of the sectional buildings of the American base, became infected by the zeal for building and proceeded to reconstruct it as a Scout Hall. This work being accomplished to their satisfaction, there was yet another hall in the village.

Work in connection with the building of the Public Hall proceeded rapidly. The day of laying the foundation stone was a memorable one. Lady Hamilton very charmingly performed the ceremony. Sir Daniel Hamilton, one of the principal donors to the funds, was there in happy mood. In his interesting speech he piously hoped that no alcoholic liquor would ever be consumed within the walls of the hall. What, were they not to enjoy themselves !

The erection was completed, and the great day of the formal opening arrived. A concert was held. Scotland was scoured for talent. Margrat Duncan and Kenneth Macrae travelled specially from Glasgow, and Duncan Morison—not yet discovered by Lady Londonderry—crossed from Stornoway. It was a great occasion.

More funds were needed as there still remained a debt on the hall. Sir Harry Lauder, a frequent visitor to the district, promised his aid. Another concert was arranged. Local artistes provided the first half of the programme ; then Sir Harry took the floor. For a whole hour he sang and danced and talked, while the crowded audience laughed and cried, and laughed again with tears in their eyes. That was a night.

Since its erection, the public hall has been in constant use. During the winter months it is used for concerts, dances, and whist drives. Badminton and billiards are other recreations. A Dramatic Society meets frequently, its members producing several new plays each winter and competing, with considerable success, at the local and national drama festivals.

Each autumn an exhibition of Highland village industries is held in the hall.   Mrs. Murray of Lochcarron and Mr. J. Hosack, J.P., Kyle, are the joint secretaries who shoulder most of the work of organisation.   The hall is filled with home-spun tweeds, knitted stockings, and various home-made garments, walking sticks, and other articles of local craftsmanship.   There is also produce of the croft, such as butter, eggs, honey, fruit, and vegetables.

The Exhibition is the fashionable event which marks the close of the tourist season.   Shooting-tenants and their house parties come to see and buy.   Private cars and 'buses bring large numbers.   Yachts anchor in the bay ; a special train arrives from the east.

The Public Hall was a necessity at the time of a Parliamentary election.   Indeed, at the by-election of 1938—when I had the pleasure of presiding at a meeting of Mr. Randolph Churchill, the Conservative candidate— we found the hall much too small.

A year previously I had stood on the platform with the one-time Radical member, Sir Ian Macpherson.   Now Sir Ian had become Baron Strathcarron, and the feudal fumes had gone to his head.   He had actually nominated his successor, an action which was later to be aped by a continental " leader."   But in our country the outward forms of democracy have to be observed, so the farce of an election went on.

My clansman had received the support of Conservative and Liberal electors ; but on this occasion four candidates had come forward.   These were English Conservative,

Welsh Liberal, Clydeside Labour, and Lossiemouth-to-London All-Party.

The evening of Mr. Churchill's meeting arrived. We drove to the hall, where a band of young men—members of the Labour Party—were waiting. These sporting youths carried Mr. Churchill shoulder high right into the hall and on to the platform. The whole audience, regardless of party, cheered enthusiastically.

And what an audience ! The hall had been filled long before the advertised time of the meeting. Every seat was occupied ; children squatted on the floor at the front, at the rear a surging mass was closely packed.

Tumultuous cheering again greeted the candidate as he rose to speak. He spoke eloquently, fluently, dramatically. He had the gift of oratory. He had personality. He swayed the audience. They listened spellbound. The lady who came to scoff, remained behind—to help him on with his overcoat.

But when polling-day came, they did not all vote for him. Canny Scots, they counted the cost. To have had Randolph Churchill as our Member would have meant enlarging the Public Hall or building a new one !

16

THE CAPITAL OF SKYE

WHETHER one goes by land or sea, a visit to Portree is a delightful trip, always provided that the weather conditions are favourable. I remember visiting it once during what can only be described as the rainy season. It was shortly after the ending of the Great War, and steamer sailings were still abnormally few.

The ferryboat to Kyleakin was unable to call at the usual pier owing to storm, so I had to go on board at the railway pier, reaching the boat by an apparently interminable climb down a perpendicular iron ladder. There was little shelter on board, and in the brief crossing the sea swept right across, thoroughly drenching the passengers.

When I reached Kyleakin I found a car waiting to take me to Portree. It was my old friend, Mr. Hay, who had taken me on my first visit to Elgol. I verily believe it was the same car, too, and the passing years had not dealt too kindly by it. It was an open car, but on this wet day Mr. Hay had put up the hood so that it was, theoretically, closed. All I can say with regard to this theory is that I wished I had taken an umbrella with me.

I do not propose to describe that journey. It is sufficient to state that it rained the whole way there, all the time I was there, and all the way back.

> " Rain, rain, glistening rain !
> Bidding us to hope again."

If the poet is right, then Skye is indeed a land of hope !

On the occasion I am about to describe, the weather was all that could be desired. It was a perfect afternoon as I set out to visit the capital of Skye by the old route. Walking down to the boat, I overtook Mr. Philip Campbell, our most recently appointed postmaster. Like several of his predecessors, Mr. Campbell had come from the east, but he had quickly got into our easy-going ways ; so now he was out, as he described it, " for a mouthful of fresh air."

Kyle is the head post office for a widely scattered area. It serves places as far apart as Ardvasar, Broadford, and

Elgol in Skye, and Arnisdale and Applecross on the mainland. There are sub-offices in remote clachans and larger ones in the villages. In course of his duties the postmaster visits all those places ; then, after a few years, when he has got to know the personnel and conditions, he is transferred elsewhere.

Fortunately there is a permanent member who takes charge during absences of the itinerant heads. She is Miss Margaret Campbell, a very capable and charming overseer who joined the staff when she left school. Recently she visited Buckingham Palace to receive a medal—well-deserved, if economical, reward for faithful service.

When Mr. Campbell and I reached the station we were told that the train would be late—a not unusual occurrence. A goods train was being unloaded at the passenger platform. Sandy Grant, the capable foreman, was urging his staff to more speed. Mr. Grant hails from Morayshire and has an absurd mania for work.

" Get a move on, boys," he was urging.

" What's all your hurry ? " was the reply, " Rome wasn't built in a day."

" Maybe not," was Sandy's quick retort, " But I wasn't foreman on that job."

Just then, Mr. MacDonald, the shipping agent, joined us. I waited for the sparks to fly. Surely a MacDonald and a Campbell could not remain at peace for long. But this afternoon the weather must have had a mellowing influence. Mr. MacDonald was in reminiscent mood, and regaled us with some of his experiences among the Western Isles. Perhaps one will be sufficient here.

A herd of cattle was being driven on board the boat at Islay. Some were unwilling, but Peter Og, a well-

K

known character who worked on the pier, had a way with him. He would take a hold of the tail, give it a twist, and the animal would sprint away.

On this occasion—so Mr. MacDonald assured us—one poor calf had had an accident to its tail. Peter Og did not know this. He grasped the creature's tail, gave it a sharp twist, and the tail came off in his hand ! Invoking the Deity—in Gaelic—the astonished man thrust the severed member inside his jersey, and calmly continued with his work. What a tale !

The *Lochmor* normally plies between Kyle and Mallaig on the Mainland, and ports in the Outer Hebrides, but on certain days during the tourist season, when the Skye boat makes special cruises to Loch Coruisk, the *Lochmor* carries passengers and mails to Portree.

So on this occasion I found Captain Robertson on the bridge. Of medium height, but more ample girth, the captain is a genial, cheery salt. Popular with passengers and crew, he has delighted many listeners to his radio talks. His distinctive voice has come breezily over the air as he has recited some incident about an inquisitive ship's cook or an inebriated sailor.

Captain Robertson has a ready wit, Some years ago, before he commanded his present ship, he was Captain of the s.s. *Plover*. The wireless operator was Mr. Douglas Macrae. I do not think that the Captain, at that time, approved of wireless. It was too newfangled for a conservative Highlander.

Then the *Shiela* disaster occurred. The Stornoway boat, *Shiela*, on her way south one morning, ran aground on the coast north of Applecross, and sent out signals of distress by radio. The *Plover* was in the harbour at Kyle and Mr. Macrae answered the signals and remained on duty continuously for a considerable time. The Captain voiced his appreciation in his own inimitable way. He just smiled whimsically, and remarked,

" If you keep a thing for seven years, you will find a use for it."

At last the train arrived. Passengers crowded on board. And what a crowd ! Ancient dowagers who had apparently selected Skye as a suitable place for wearing out their equally ancient garments. Slangy, lip-sticked shop-girls and cheery, bare-legged young women from the universities, and more elderly maiden ladies who had not yet given up hope.

And the men. Pompous, bespatted politicians mixed with respectable, care-worn business men, all equally glad to be free for a while to breathe the fresh Highland air. There were a few young men and a couple of ministers, the latter heavily coated in spite of the warm day, and carrying the inevitable umbrella. Most of the passengers were on holiday from the south. The local people mostly cross by ferry, and travel by 'bus, but the ministers prefer the boat—where the seating capacity is more ample.

The bells clanged ; ropes were let go ; we were off. Out in the bay we passed a fishery cruiser riding at anchor, the Scottish Lion rampant flying at the mast head. At one time the personal flag of Scottish kings—or so the Lyon King-at-arms alleges—this flag now indicated the presence on board of His Majesty's Secretary of State for Scotland.

During winter months the fishery cruisers patrol our coasts, preventing and detecting illegal trawling. With the arrival of summer, particularly if there is a spell of fine weather, it becomes urgently necessary for some

member of His Majesty's Government to pay a personal
visit to outlying parts of the Highlands.

We should feel grateful that Westminster can spare
her statesmen and politicians. They come, ostensibly,
to enquire into some grievance which, in the goodness of
their hearts, they desire to put right. We may wonder
that they do not use the telephone, which now penetrates
into practically every corner of the Highlands.

Leaving the cruiser behind, we sailed past the lighthouse, so near that we could almost see the smile on the
face of the lone keeper's daughter as she waved her hand.
We passed through the narrow water between Pabay and
the mainland of Skye.

Pabay, the Priest's Isle, contains the ruins of a
church and an old graveyard. There is now only one
dwelling-house on the island. Being perfectly flat,
almost square in shape, and nearly a square mile in
extent, Pabay has been used as an emergency
aerodrome.

Our first call was at Broadford, where our boat
touched at a black wooden wharf at the end of a narrow
stone pier. This wharf did not look very substantial and
it has since been closed for traffic, all passengers now
travelling by road.

Even then we noticed that there was not the same
stir at the pier as a few years earlier, before a network of
motor-omnibus services encompassed the island. We
noticed, however, that the mails were still sent by steamboat ; for the Post Office is a conservative institution !

North of Broadford lies the circular-shaped Isle of
Scalpay, about five miles in diameter. It is one of a group
which includes Longay, Pabay, and Guillaman, all the
property of Captain Muntz. The passage between

Scalpay and Skye being too shallow for navigation, we passed outside between Scalpay and Longay.

The crab-shaped Island of Crowlin loomed up on our right. Fifty years ago there were thirty people living on this isle. Now it is deserted. Shortly after the last inhabitant had crossed to the mainland, I landed by motor-boat, along with my wife and son, one Saturday evening.

Donald Mor having seen us safely ashore, turned his boat and made for his home at Kyleakin, after promising to return for us on Monday morning. Darkness was beginning to fall, and the nearest level ground was swampy and uninviting. After a hurried look round, we pitched our camp on the sloping edge of a cliff.

We passed an uneventful night although, when I awoke, my feet certainly felt a bit chilly. The slope on the hillside had caused me to slip down so that they had penetrated below the tent and were dangling over the cliff.

Our first action on rising was to hoist our flag over the camp. After breakfast we set out to explore the island. The ruins of a clachan were less than a quarter mile distant, one house still remaining almost habitable. Nearby was a well which we cleaned out. Inland there was a fresh water loch where some wild fowl were flying about listlessly. Perhaps, the day being a Sunday, these birds were not singing with their usual joyousness.

We spent a glorious day wandering all over the island. On the west side we found a natural harbour capable of sheltering fairly large ships. Along the coast we explored several caves. We had the whole island to ourselves. There were no neighbours, no Sabbatarians, no Mrs. Grundy.

Towards evening a gale arose ; the sea became

rough. Would Donald Mor manage to come for us in the morning ? We had only a limited amount of food, but so hungry were we after our day in the open, that we ate Monday's breakfast before going to bed.

Next morning we were up early, scanning the sea. We need not have worried. Donald Mor's boat was speeding towards us. Sunshine or storm, he would not have failed us. Soon we were on board, skimming rapidly over the waves, back to business and reality.

But I must leave Crowlin and its delightful memories. I am bound for Portree. To continue our cruise ! The *Lochmor* sailed westward through Kylemore at the south end of Raasay, calling at the mining pier at Suishnish Point. This is a substantial pier which was erected for the shipment of iron ore from the mines in the centre of the island

Passing through the Narrows, we entered the Sound of Raasay and continued along the coast up the west of the island. We passed Raasay House, beautifully situated near the shore, where Dr. Johnson and James Boswell had stayed. At one time the home of the Macleod of Raasay, it is now, like so many other historic Highland mansions, a tourist hotel.

During their memorable tour, Johnson and Boswell spent several days in Raasay. Boswell relates how he and three companions climbed to the top of Dun Caan, the flat-topped mountain on the south of the island, where they indulged in a Highland dance.

In 1745, Macleod of Raasay, whose family had owned the island since the fourteenth century, raised a hundred fighting men for the Prince. Now the Board of Agriculture are the proprietors, for the last Macleod of Raasay was killed in the Great War, when leading his English regiment. Neil Munro has written a poignant lament :

" Allan Ian Oig Macleod of Raasay,
   Treasure of mine, lies yonder dead in Loos,
His body unadorned by Highland raiment,
   Tramelled for glorious hours, in Saxon trews."

Our ship steamed steadily on along the coast of
Raasay and round Ben Tianavaig towards Portree Bay.
As we approached the town of Portree, rising in stately
terraces round the bay, we were impressed by the beauty
of the scene. Numerous small boats were anchored in
the bay, and several motor craft flitted to and fro. Our
ship touched the pier and, if one might judge by the sound,
was tied up in Gaelic !

Near this spot King James V had landed in 1536.
That monarch, after subduing the Chief of Macleod, had
sailed round the north of Skye and anchored his ship in
the bay. After landing he had set up his court on what
is now Portree Square. And so the town received the
name of Portree, in Gaelic *Port-righ*, meaning royal port.

To-day there are Gaelic authorities who claim that
" port of the slope " is the correct meaning of Portree.
After all, it is no use being an authority on a subject if one
is to accept the obvious explanation. Yet these experts
are so stereotyped in their methods. They simply
contradict what has long been recognised as a fact, and
proceed to build up a new theory. It is immaterial that
this theory is fantastic so long as it is different. Port of
the slope, indeed !

Two centuries after the visit of King James V, the
son of King James VIII came also to Portree. But he
did not come with the pomp of his ancestor ; he came, a
wanderer, footsore and weary. And for him there was
no room in the inn. He had to cross to Raasay for
shelter, and on his return to Skye his refuge was a cow-shed
on the outskirts of the town.

Nearly two more centuries were to elapse before the son of another king visited Portree. And he, too, wore the tartan of their common ancestor. Their Royal Highnesses the Duke and Duchess of York, during their memorable visit to Dunvegan Castle in 1933, came to declare open the Elgin Hostel for schoolboys. It was a holiday throughout Skye, and from all over the island the clans gathered at Portree to give the Royal guests a rousing welcome.

The passengers stepped ashore on to a wooden jetty. Then we all marched in single file towards a wicket guarded by a man in uniform. It was as if we were entering a foreign country, but this was not a customs official. We had landed on a private pier, and he was simply collecting toll.

The shipping company had failed to implement their promise to take us to Portree for the sum marked on our tickets. They had merely taken us alongside a privately-owned wharf ; so, before we could set foot in the capital of Skye, we had to hand over the sum of one penny. Then, it seemed, we were permitted, by courtesy of the representatives of Lord MacDonald, to walk along the depressing quayside street.

For this street, the only approach to Portree by sea, is the property of Lord MacDonald, and those who act for his lordship do not allow even a motor-omnibus to stand there. In these days of constant dictation by Government officials, it is cheering to realise that Lord MacDonald is still lord of Portree.

We approached the centre of the town by a steep climb up a winding road which leads to the Square. There was an uncomfortable air of quiet everywhere. Young men stood in small groups about street corners ;

one or two leaned against a shop doorway. It was then I noticed that all the shops were closed. I had chosen an unfortunate day for my visit. It was the Fast Day.

Yes, it was the Fast Day. All business had been suspended for the day. There was an air of deep Sabbath gloom, and I felt that I ought not to be sight-seeing on such a day. Truth to tell, there was not much to see ; for Portree, seen close at hand, does not appear so attractive as when viewed from the sea. And the Fast Day did nothing to brighten it up !

Presbyterians had been singularly lacking in foresight when they discarded the Saints' Days of the Old Religion, and set up in their place the so-called Fast Days. Different days had been appointed for different parishes, and the plan probably worked satisfactorily at first ; but with the advent of the railway, the system broke down in all but the most remote corners of the country. It was impossible to run a train if there had to be complete cessation of work in some parish through which it ran.

In Skye there are no railways, so there are still observed Fast Days, Thanksgiving Days, and even Days of Humiliation. On such days all work stops. Elderly men and women dress in sombre raiment, and gather together to listen to sonorous discourses and ponderous denunciations of evil-doers. It is a cheering thought that the evil is usually that of rival denominations !

Portree is not a town in the sense of being a burgh, but it is the seat of a sheriff court ; not, I understand, a very busy one. For the morals of Portree are well looked after, if one may judge by the number of places of worship.

St. Columba's Scottish Episcopal Church is perhaps the most interesting one. Here Canon MacCulloch, author of *The Misty Isle of Skye,* was rector for a number of years. It contains a stained glass window, dedicated to the memory of Flora MacDonald. The inscription reads :

TO THE GLORY OF GOD AND IN MEMORY OF FLORA MACDONALD,

DAUGHTER OF RANALD THE SON OF ANGUS MACDONALD THE YOUNGER, MILTON, SOUTH UIST. SHE WAS BORN IN 1722, AND WAS MARRIED NOVEMBER 6th, 1750, AT FLODIGARRY, ISLE OF SKYE, TO ALLAN VII IN DESCENT OF THE KINGS-BURGH MACDONALDS, CAPTAIN 34th ROYAL HIGHLAND EMIGRANT REGIMENT, WHO SERVED WITH DISTINCTION THROUGH THE AMERICAN WAR OF INDEPENDENCE. SHE DIED MARCH 5th, 1790, AND WAS BURIED AT KILMUIR, ISLE OF SKYE. SHE EFFECTED THE ESCAPE OF PRINCE CHARLES EDWARD FROM SOUTH UIST AFTER THE BATTLE OF CULLODEN IN 1746 ; AND IN 1779, WHEN RETURNING FROM AMERICA ON BOARD A SHIP ATTACKED BY A FRENCH PRIVATEER, ENCOURAGED THE SAILORS TO MAKE A SPIRITED AND SUCCESSFUL RESISTANCE, THUS RISKING HER LIFE FOR BOTH THE HOUSES OF STUART AND HANOVER. THIS WINDOW WAS DEDICATED TO THE MEMORY OF FLORA MACDONALD IN THE YEAR OF OUR LORD 1896 BY ONE OF HER GREAT GRAND-CHILDREN, FANNY CHARLOTTE, WIDOW OF LIEUTENANT-COLONEL R. E. HENRY, AND DAUGH-TER OF JAMES MURRAY MACDONALD, GRANDSON OF FLORA MACDONALD.

17

LOCH CORUISK

ON a visit to Edinburgh some years ago, I was struck by the presence of a number of old horse-cabs, of the " growler " type, lined up on Princes Street. My wife turned down a suggestion that we should have a run in one. She refused to risk her life in a horse-drawn vehicle. I was told that the cabs were there to provide " atmosphere " for the American tourist.

A similar reason may be adduced for the use, until recently, of Highland ponies to carry tourists to Loch Coruisk. Those sure-footed little animals could find their way along Glen Sligachan in torrential rain or thickest mist ; for, no matter how fine the weather when one sets out through the mountains, there is always the possibility of being caught in a downpour or wrapped in invisibility.

Formerly only the well-to-do could afford the time and expense of a trip by horseback ; so this gem, shut away in the heart of the Cuillins, was hidden from the sight of all but a select few. But motor-transport has changed this, and now thousands of tourists of all classes visit the famous loch each summer. Some go by private car or char-a-banc to Elgol where motor boats, large and small, are waiting to carry them across Loch Scavaig. Others travel by one of the MacBrayne boats which makes periodic cruises round the south of the island.

The " Lord of the Isles " was waiting on the pier as I crossed to Skye. For such was the name which Mr. Skinner had given to his smart char-a-banc. The morning was warm and bright, so each seat was quickly occupied.

135

Soon we had left Kyleakin and were speeding across the moors. We slowed down a little as we turned west at Broadford, but the road surface remained passable until Torrin was reached. Beyond that, we held on to the sides of the vehicle and trusted to fate—and the driver.

The scene at Elgol resembled a market day. There were numerous char-a-bancs from Broadford and Portree, and private cars from every corner of the island. Our 'bus had stopped at the top of the hill, near the house of Mrs. Mackinnon where I had been entertained on the occasion of my visit to the Spar Cave. But Mrs. Mackinnon had passed on. It was her son who met us, for he is now one of the principal boat-owners. He had left one of his hands in Flanders some years earlier, but he can make good use of the other. It can not only use an oar, but it can use a pen—as several recalcitrant pensions' officials have learnt.

Many of the crofters were busy in the harvest field, the men wielding the scythe and the women gathering the corn and binding the sheaves. Formerly the women had cut the corn with the *corran* or sickle, but now the scythe is almost universally used. In the old days the soil was tilled by means of the *cas-crom* (crooked spade), but now this has mostly given place to the plough ; although there are still many patches of land among the rocks where the old implement is more serviceable.

Elgol is one of the places in Skye where Gaelic is still spoken, especially among the older people ; and, as elsewhere throughout the island, there is a large proportion of elderly men and women. These will sometimes tell you that they " have not got the English very good," yet they speak the language more fluently and comprehensibly than many Lowlanders.

Some years ago an English lady, visiting this part of

Skye, was greatly charmed by the sweet voices and fresh appearance of the young women. She persuaded one rosy-faced girl named Bella Mackinnon to return with her to London as children's nurse. She wanted her two little boys to hear the softly spoken English of the Highland lass, in preference to the harsher accents of the Cockney.

At the same time she looked forward to the pleasure she would derive from impressing this humble girl from the wilds of Skye with the magnificence of London. She did not know the Highland character. Few suffer from inferiority complex !

Bella liked London. She made an ideal nurse. She saw many things which must have been strange to her, but never did she utter a word of surprise. One evening her mistress took her to listen to a world-famous singer. Bella sat mute throughout.

When they reached home the mistress said to Bella, " Wasn't that a marvellous voice ? I am sure you never heard such wonderful singing before."

Bella was not prepared to admit superiority in anything.

" It's myself will be thinking," she answered, " there's a girl I know in Elgol who could beat her if only she had the training."

We accompanied Mr. Mackinnon down the steep winding track to the shore. It was high tide, and a small boat lay waiting in a narrow creek. This inlet had been fashioned partly by nature, but, in addition, a number of boulders had been built to form a makeshift pier, only serviceable however at high water. At other states of the tide, passengers had to wade through the surf or be carried on board by one of the boatmen.

" The Government ought to build a pier for us," I

was told. It is always the same cry. The Government
is expected to do everything. Certainly a pier would be
advantageous not only to the inhabitants but also to the
visitor, but its absence should not be regarded as entirely
a drawback. To many, the difficulties of approach are
part of the charm. Once Loch Coruisk becomes too
easily accessible, the desire to visit it will tend to disappear.

The boatmen rowed us, in several small parties, to
the motor skiff anchored in the bay. Soon we were all on
board and our vessel ploughing through the waves.
There was a stiff breeze, but the day was bright and, in
radio phraseology, " visibility good." To the west, some
three miles distant, the Isle of Soay showed up clearly.
Farther south we could see the outlines of Canna and Rum.

Our boat steered north. On our left lay the narrow
Sound of Soay, and beyond it rose Rudh an Dunain
guarding the entrance to Loch Brittle. On our right
Ben Meabost towered above Elgol. Nearer the shore
stretched the path to Camasunary. We passed the " bad
step," really one of the attractions of the path, and only a
danger to those who try to avoid it.

The approach to the head of Loch Scavaig is guarded
by several islets covered with birch and wild flowers.
Steering past these, our boat drew near the rocky coast
then with a gentle scraping of the keel came to rest along
side a projecting ledge. We quickly scrambled ashore, ready
to set out for Loch Coruisk, only a quarter mile inland.

The boatmen turned the boat and, as it moved off
Mackinnon shouted cheerily,

" I'll be back for you in a couple of hours."

He had gone back for a meal, or perhaps to seek
another load of passengers. One of our party, Mr. Brown
of London, we called him, took out his watch.

" Let me see," he said, " it's ten to twelve now. We'll meet here at ten to two."

Mr. Brown was a very capable, matter-of-fact business man. To him, an hour meant sixty minutes, neither more nor less. His education was to develop !

We scattered a little as we made our way to Coruisk. Some paused to admire the great peaks rising to the skies, or to watch some waterfall as it plunged to the depths,

> " Where a wild stream with headlong shock,
> Came brawling down its bed of rock,
> To mingle with the main."

We reached the loch, that gem of creation. Giant boulders guarded the shore. All around towered the jagged peaks of the Cuillins ; the peak of Charles, the peak of Alexander, the Peak of Norman ; Black Peak, Red Peak, Notched Peak ; Peak of Young Men and Peak of Mighty Winds.

The loch stretches northward into the heart of the mountains. A small island near the shore presented a patch of colour, but the waters themselves looked dark, deep, and forbidding. We stood for a little on that desolate shore which Scott has immortalised :

> " For rarely human eye has known
> A scene so stern as that dread lake,
> With its dark ledge of barren stone."

Mr. Brown was already looking at his watch ; he must not be late for his appointment. This recalled me to reality. I had gone there to get some photographs.

Although not a mountaineer, I found it necessary to climb up the hillside in order to reach suitable view-points. The result was that, when I got back to the landing-place, all the other members of our party had already collected.

I fancied that Mr. Brown looked at me reproachfully.
Perhaps I was half an hour late, but at anyrate the boat
was not yet in sight. As it happened, we had to wait a
considerable time before it appeared.

We sat on that rocky shore waiting, afraid to go far
away in case the boat should come and depart in our
absence, leaving us stranded. Those who knew and loved
the Highlands waited contentedly, enjoying every moment.
They remained there, breathing in the ozone and basking
in the sunshine.

But there were others who had gone there simply
because it happened to be the fashion. The beauty of
mountain and loch was wasted on them. To such people,
even the sight of a mountain deer merely suggested a
hat-rack. They did not want to feast on scenery ; they
hungered for something more satisfying. Awful thought,
if the boat did not come soon, they might be late for
dinner !

At last the overdue vessel arrived. Mr. Mackinnon
had secured a fresh batch of passengers, and he came
ashore with them. We waited ready to go on board.
Mr. Mackinnon was smiling. He had enjoyed a good meal,
and business was brisk. But Mr. Brown's face was like
thunder. He stood, watch in hand, while we gathered
round.

He told Mr. Mackinnon that he was exactly one hour
and forty-two minutes late, and that we seventeen people
had been kept waiting there for that period. He went on
to enumerate in great detail further facts to which he
attached great importance. He puffed out his chest, he
waxed eloquent as he pictured to Mackinnon the depths
of infamy to which he had descended in keeping us there.
He wound up as he had begun :

" You promised to be here in two hours' time, and you have taken exactly three hours and forty-two minutes. What do you mean by it ? "

Mr. Mackinnon smiled. He turned his eyes to the great mountains he loved. He glanced at Mr. Brown of London, and there was pity in that look. Then he answered, slowly and serenely,

" Indeed, and it's many a one would be delighted to have the chance of spending an extra hour or two here ! "

18

OUR MINISTERS

" MORTALS, buy of me ; I am the only one which deals with the truth ; all the others are impostors." This, wrote Voltaire, was the cry of two hundred sects of Christianity.

Two hundred sects ! In Kyle we have reduced the number to three ; yet each member of these is firmly convinced that his particular denomination alone is right. There is a satisfying feeling in looking mournfully—from a non-contaminable distance—at our erring brothers, as we breathe the smug prayer, " Thank God, we are not as other men are."

Kyle is the ecclesiastical centre of the north-west of Scotland, and for many years the Synod of Glenelg met here annually. The Synod is the second highest court of the Church of Scotland, it being next in importance to the General Assembly which sits in Edinburgh.

When the Church of Scotland and the United Free

L

Church became reunited, the Synod was transferred to Dingwall; but the Free Church—that pillar of stability—adheres staunchly to its former meeting-place. Presbytery meetings of all three churches are held periodically, with the result that on certain days there are more ministers than laymen to be seen.

It is interesting to observe the mannerisms and peculiarities of dress associated with each particular denomination. You see one minister, cheery of countenance, with a full Roman collar; you see a sad-looking divine wearing a similar article almost apologetically.

Again, you see a minister in deepest black, carrying a baggy umbrella already unfolded as if its owner eternally feared the worst. And this type wears a white starched collar and a white bow tie. Bands of purity, symbols of piety!

There was a time when the minister ruled his flock, but to-day, probably due to the spread of schism and dissent, the congregations too often rule their ministers. The extremists, in religion as in politics, are always the most active and vitriolic.

Then there are Sabbatarian fanatics who have never heard the command to labour for six days. These good people are only concerned with the day of rest. Rest from what, one wonders.

Some years ago I attended a public meeting called to protest against the running of Sunday trains. There was a large gathering consisting mainly of ministers and middle-aged or elderly women. All had a well-fed if rather stern appearance. Two pressmen were also present. Less rotund in appearance, they looked considerably more cheerful.

The public meeting opened with the singing of a

metrical psalm, a proceeding which had a noticeably subduing effect on the scribes. Several lengthy prayers followed, after which the chairman, the Very Reverend Finlay Macrae, ex-Moderator of the Free Church, explained the purpose of the meeting.

Several ministers spoke. They rambled on, apparently quoting copiously and quite irrelevantly from sermons they had preached during the preceding fifty years. Yet when one pressman ventured to speak, he was immediately ruled out of order.

Although, as I have stated, the meeting was called specifically to discuss the running of Sunday trains, the word " Sunday " was not mentioned by any of the clerical speakers. For this is a word which, in our beautiful Highlands, may only be uttered by Papists, Atheists, and Evildoers !

If you hope for salvation you must say " Sabbath," and if you feel particularly sanctimonious you may say " Saw-bath." Surely the miserable, under-fed journalist, who asked the chairman if he meant the seventh-day Sabbath of the Bible, could not have realised his wickedness in asking such a question.

Before he could be shouted down, he went on to ask at what time the new day began, seeing that Kyle of Lochalsh was situated several degrees west of Greenwich. He asked if the Sabbath was to be reckoned by the clock or the sun.

The chairman was a man of peace. He was having no argument. " We are not here to discuss matters of that kind," he informed his questioner. However, in these pagan days the last word lies with the Press which duly reported that the chairman was unable to provide guidance on the subject.

Towards the end of a long drawn-out, if one-sided, discussion, a motion condemning the running of Sunday trains was put to the meeting and carried. An amendment, objecting to all unnecessary vehicular traffic on Sunday, had found no seconder. For among the most rabid of the anti-Sunday train element there were several car-owners! Anyway, who bothers nowadays about being consistent?

One minister, well-known in the district, whose absence from that meeting was remarked, was the Reverend D. T. Mackay. Mr. Mackay did not concern himself with worldly trivialities and controversies. At that moment he was probably giving comfort to some poor or ailing person.

" D.T.," as he was affectionately called, did not bother about religious denominations. He would preach in any church. It was immaterial whether the pulpit was on the right side or the left. Failing a church being available for a service, he would preach in a school, a hall or even a barn. When Hebridean fisher girls went east to Yarmouth, he followed them, preaching to them in their own tongue, and generally seeing to their welfare.

> " A man was he to all the country dear,
> And passing rich with forty pounds a year.
> Remote from town, he ran his godly race
> Nor e'er had changed nor wished to change his place."

Numerous stories are told about " D.T."—perhaps some have become exaggerated with the passage of time. On one occasion, when conducting Communion services in the Outer Isles, he was obliged to share a bed with a fellow-minister. D.T. did not mind this—he could sleep anywhere. He made it a rule to go to bed late and rise early. This gave him more time for his life's work.

When he retired at last, his bedfellow was apparently asleep. What was D.T.'s horror to find his foot touching an ice-cold leg! He jumped at once from bed, went down on his knees and prayed lengthily and fervently. Presently a voice from the bed enquired drowsily if he was nearly finished.

D.T. cried out, " Praise the Lord. He's alive again ! " Then followed an ardent prayer of thankfulness before he was at last persuaded to return to bed.

Next day it was obviously useless for the hostess to explain. In actual fact, an earthenware hot water bottle had been left cold in bed by mistake. The touch of this cold bottle had misled D.T. However he was satisfied that his prayers had prevailed, and that a miracle had been wrought.

One day I happened to be talking to Mr. Charles Manson, and in course of conversation D.T.'s name was mentioned. Charlie's face lit up instantly.

" I must tell you a story about him," he said. Mr. Manson is an engine-driver and one of our most worthy townsmen, although it must be admitted that he is not a churchgoer. He says that he has no use for ministers.

" I was driving the five o'clock train from Kyle one evening," he began, " and I noticed D.T. leaving his compartment as the train stopped at Plockton, so I thought I would save him a long walk by offering to stop the train at Duncraig platform."

" I thought you did not like ministers," I pointed out.

" Ministers ! " said Charlie, " D.T. is more than a minister. He's a Christian." I was squashed.

" Was D.T. pleased ? " I persisted.

" Pleased," said Charlie, and chuckled quietly, " I don't know ; but he wasn't very complimentary about the speed of our trains. He just answered, ' No, no, I'll walk. I'm in a hurry ! ' "

The Rev. N. C. Macdonald, whose charge is the West Church, Plockton, is of a different type. Tall, lean, ascetic, he spends much time in study. On Sundays he provides a well-reasoned, learned discourse, a mental and moral stimulant. I have heard visitors remark that he ought to be minister of a city charge. Presumably the pews of our city churches are overflowing with intellectuals.

There are critics who disapprove of ministers " wasting " time in study. These good people would have the parson spending his days going from house to house drinking tea with his parishioners, and of course visiting the slums.

Slums ! There need be no slums in a civilized country. If we had statesmen, instead of self-centred, fossilised platitudinarians, decent houses could be built for every family, work found for the unemployed, and slums wiped from the land.

Last century, even before the date of Queen Victoria's visit to Loch Maree, the Government awoke to the need for more churches for the Highlands. So an Act of Parliament was passed by which portions of certain populous districts were separated from the existing civil parishes. These new charges, of which Plockton was one, were called *Quoad Sacra* parishes.

The first incumbent of Plockton whom I remember was the Rev. John Mackay. I have already mentioned him as being an unwitting recipient of the Kyle Hotel bounty. He was succeeded in his charge by the Rev. Samuel Nicolson, who is still with us.

Mr. Nicolson is, however, far from being still. Indeed,

for a Highland minister, he is exceptionally active. He has been for many years a member of the County Council. He has also held office as Parish Councillor and member of the Education Committee and similar bodies. He is a man who knows his own mind. If he disagrees with you, he has no hesitation in saying so. I fancy he enjoys the telling.

The principal Higher Grade school in the west of the county is at Plockton. Some years after Mr. Nicolson came to reside there, I was discussing the school problem with him. I argued that, as the ministers found Kyle a convenient centre for Synod and Presbytery meetings, parents considered it to be equally suitable as a centre for Higher education.

To clinch my argument, I pointed out that it was absurd to have a Higher Grade school at Plockton, a village where there had not been a single birth for six years.

Mr. Nicolson answered me in all seriousness : " Oh, that has been all altered since I came."

A large portion of the civil parish of Lochalsh has been retained as the ecclesiastical parish ; in addition, Killilan, a part of Kintail hallowed by St. Filan, has been added. The minister is the Rev. John Maclean, a quiet, dignified, and scholarly bachelor with just sufficient trace of Highland accent to prove attractive to the visitor. He has been blessed with a rare fund of humour, a gift which, owing to his environment, he must necessarily restrain— especially in the pulpit.

All the ministers in the parish, including those of the Free Presbyterian and Free Churches, conduct occasional services at Kyle where the Church of Scotland has a resident missionary. Those missionaries usually remain for a period of three years before passing on to their next charge.   Although belonging to a church which likes to be regarded as very democratic, they are, in actual fact, sent up to the Highlands in accordance with the whim of a worthy divine residing in Edinburgh.

On one occasion this spiritual autocrat sent a letter, intimating to the local congregation that he was sending along a missionary who had spent many years among the heathen in darkest Africa and was " eminently suited for such a place as Kyle of Lochalsh ! "

The missionary was due to arrive.   An elder went to the railway station to welcome him.   It was the evening train, and passengers were few.   He walked up to a likely-looking individual.

" Are you the new missionary ? " he enquired.

" No," was the startled reply of the passenger, who, it transpired later, was a commercial traveller.   " No, I'm not a missionary.   It is indigestion that makes my face like this."

Mr. George Thomson, our ex-African missionary, appeared in due course.   His tales were refreshing.   On one occasion he had found a native badly beaten up in a tribal quarrel.   He put a poultice on his head, bandaged him, and hoped for the best.   Next morning he called to enquire about the patient, half expecting to hear that he was dead.   But no, Sambo's head was thick.   He was sitting up, calmly eating his poultice.

I must admit that Mr. Thomson's experiences were at times reminiscent of similar stories I had read ; which only goes to prove that there is nothing new even under the African sun.

Although this record must necessarily be brief, there is one minister whose name I cannot omit.   He is the Rev.

Alexander Mactaggart, M.A., Minister-emeritus of Glenelg. He was for many years clerk of the Synod of Glenelg and is still clerk to the Presbytery of Lochcarron.

Chairmen of Synods and Presbyteries are called moderators. These hold office usually for a period of one year, but the clerk is, in practice, a permanent official. It is he who keeps everyone right. He is secretary, law-agent, and counsellor. Others may shirk their duty, but not he.

The parish of Glenelg is only six miles distant by sea, and as a rule Mr. Mactaggart travelled to Kyle by boat. There are times when the sea is too stormy to cross, and on one such occasion a number of years ago he had to come by road.

He set out in his pony trap, up the Great Glen at Glenelg. Minister and horse made their way deter-minedly along Glenmore and over Mam Ratagan, the piercing gale sometimes threatening to lift them bodily from the ground. Slowly they drove along the winding road and down the steep mountainside towards Loch Duich. They were retracing the steps of Samuel Johnson and Boswell, those great pioneers of a century and a half earlier.

Mr. Mactaggart's route lay round the head of Loch Duich, past Inverinate, and on to the ferry at Dornie. Minister and horse and trap were ferried across the turbulent loch, and the journey resumed.

Next day Mr. Mactaggart, clerk to the Presbytery, appeared at the meeting prompt to the minute. He had travelled thirty miles by road to get there. Like Emerson, he must have felt that the reward of a thing well done was to have done it.

This sense of duty is ingrained in our Highland

ministers. People who do not understand may criticise, but deep down beneath the veneer of sectarianism you will find them kindly, helpful, and generous. There is the same welcome for the wandering gypsy as for the more affluent laird. The Manse keeps open door for all.

Yet the Church is a poorly paid profession. The minister gives his services free for baptism, marriage, or funeral. Even the proclamation of banns costs the victim only a few shillings. In fact, the only way to spend money on getting married in Scotland is by going to the Registrar's Office.

19

ORD AND ARMADALE

ALTHOUGH motor-buses now run to most parts of Skye, there are still a number of beauty spots on the island almost unspoilt by the breath of petrol. It was to some of those peaceful retreats, well off the beaten track, that I set out along with Roddy Cameron one bright summer day. Roddy drove an up-to-date car, and he knew how to make it go. When with him I never experienced the least anxiety lest anyone should run into us—from behind.

A splendid driver, Roddy was also an excellent companion. He was not one of those stiff-necked, narrow-minded individuals who are always ready to contradict. On the contrary, Roddy was out to please. Never at a loss for an answer, what he did not know he extemporised as circumstances necessitated.

I had left home with the intention of getting some photographs and, conditions being favourable, we halted near Breakish for the first picture. Setting up my camera on its stand by the roadside, I waited a short time for a fleeting cloud to drift into position over Broadford. Just then an old man sauntered up and, speaking in English, bade me " Good morning." He then turned to Roddy and carried on an animated conversation in Gaelic.

When we resumed our journey, I saw that Roddy appeared to be particularly well satisfied with himself.

" The old man asked what you were doing," he volunteered at length, " so I just told him you were taking levels for the new water supply."

" What on earth made you say that ? " I asked.

" Oh, well," he replied, " the Breakish people have been asking the County Council to give them a new water supply, so I wanted to cheer the old chap up."

A kindly thought !

When we reached Crossroads we turned off the main road, keeping due south to Armadale. The name Crossroads seems inappropriate, as the roads do not cross but meet as at the junction of the arms of a capital Y. Our car skimmed over that moorland road in record time. The first habitations we passed were at Drumfearn, where green patches on the hillside indicated the presence of a small crofting township.

Black scars on the purple moor marked the places where peat banks had been cut ; for peat is still used to a considerable extent in the rural parts of the island. The work of preparing this cheap fuel is most interesting, and whole families turn out to help.

A special spade, called *torr-sgian* in Gaelic, is used to cut the soft peats which are laid out in rows to dry.

Small heaps, called *rubhan* in Gaelic, are built, each heap having five peats upstanding and one laid across the top. The peats are left to dry and harden in the sun, and then built into stacks ready for taking home.

Formerly the peats were carried home in creels on the backs of the women and older children ; now-a-days they are usually taken to the roadside, ready to be brought home by horse and cart or even by motor lorry. They are then built into stacks near the dwelling-house, the prudent householder each autumn storing sufficient peats to last a year.

Farther on we approached Duisdale House, beautifully situated among trees and now a tourist hotel for which it was well adapted. A short distance beyond, a narrow road branches off to the village of Isleornsay, quaint, picturesque, and old-world in appearance, but possessing a very comfortable hotel.

Isleornsay pier might have been the original of the one described by George A. Birmingham in *General John Regan*. Certainly on the day I saw it, the sea was noticeably at a distance.

The lighthouse is built on an ebb-tide isle, which may be reached by land at low water. Across the Sound is Loch Hourn, a deep, wild loch surrounded by high mountains and known as the Loch of Hell. Fifty years ago several members of a fishing crew, including one man now residing at Kyle of Lochalsh, saw a strange monster rear itself high out of the waters of the loch.

According to legend, Loch Hourn and Loch Ness are connected by a subterranean passage. It may be that the " Lochness Monster," which is only visible in the waters of the Ness during the holiday period, spends the remainder of the year at Loch Hourn.

Above Isleornsay the road curves inland past Camuscross to Loch nan Dubrachan. Here we turned off the main road and followed the narrow hill road leading to Ord. Our car sped across the moor, then slowed down as we penetrated Glen Meodal and skirted the river till we reached the sea at Ord.

Ord House occupies a commanding position near the shore. Alexander Smith stayed there when he wrote his Skye classic, *A Summer in Skye*. And surely there was no spot on this enchanted isle more fitted to give inspiration. Across the sky-line, beyond Loch Eishort, stretch the Cuillins ; and away to the west, basking in the shimmering Atlantic, lie the islands of Rum and Canna.

The road stretches along the coast to Tockavaig. All around there was wonderful colouring and profusion of foliage. The whole scene was one vast rock garden, a description of which might have taxed even the powers of Shakespeare when he wrote :

> " I know a bank whereon the wild thyme blows,
> Where ox-lips and the nodding violet grows,
> Quite over-canopied with lush woodbine
> With sweet musk roses and with eglantine."

A number of Highland cattle were grazing along the roadside, and as I approached Tockavaig I noticed one magnificent specimen in a field there. I judged it would look well in the foreground of a photograph, so I crossed the fence, walked along the field to a suitable position, and opened out my camera.

Now I had always heard that these Highland cattle were quiet, inoffensive animals. Besides, I was brought up on a farm. In fact, my father at one time owned a herd of these wild Highlanders, although I fancy he kept them more for sentiment than financial gain.

Our farm was on the far north of Aberdeenshire, and again I fancy it was chosen more for scenery than profit ; certainly it was an oasis in that utilitarian county.   It must have been heartening for my father to walk along the glen, admiring those shaggy brown cattle with their magnificent horns, and picturing himself once more in the land of his youth.

So now, having my camera fixed up, I was not perturbed when the animal approached. My only concern was that it might slobber over me, and, to prevent this discomfort, I put out my hand to pat it on the head . . .

I was lying flat on my back, in a perfectly straight line. How I reached the ground I do not know ; but there I lay, undamaged camera in hand, with that magnificent beast towering above me.

" Stay where you are," I heard.

The advice was superfluous.   I was feeling absolutely happy.   I was having a glorious rest, without care or worry.   But Roddy was determined to rescue me.   He came with a stick, and distracted the shaggy brute's attention while I, still a bit dazed, retraced my steps to the car.

" That must have been a wild one," said Roddy, after he had followed me back.   " I expect that was why it was put into the field behind a fence," he added, wise after the event.

Near the shore, some distance from the roadway, stand the ruins of the prehistoric Castle of Dunscaith. As I set out to walk over to it, Roddy came along too, carrying a stick.

" I see some cattle over there," he remarked, " I am coming with you in case there are any more wild ones."

Dunskaith Castle had been built on a rock, separated from the land by a narrow gorge across which a drawbridge had provided the only access. At a later date a narrow roadway had been built, supported by a stone archway. At the time I visited the ruins, the crown of the archway had fallen in and an old railway sleeper provided the only means of crossing.

We climbed to the castle ramparts, now grass-covered. Across Loch Eishort there is a wonderful view. To the north the Red Hills stand up, and in the distance, beyond Loch Slapin, Glamaig, Marsco and Blaven can be seen. Westward across Strathaird rise the great peaks of the Cuillins.

Several sheep were grazing peacefully on the top of the castle rock. It was of this quiet spot that Alexander Smith wrote :

> " Upon a ruin by the desert shore
> I sat one Autumn day of utter peace
> Watching a lustrous stream of vapour pour
> O'er Blaaven, fleece on fleece."

Beyond Dunskaith we followed the road inland above Tarskavaig Point, descending again to the shore at Tarskavaig Bay. Here, where a mountain stream comes tumbling down to the sea, are several sheltered sandy coves ideally suited for camping and bathing.

We continued along the side of the stream to Dougal's Loch. Down by the burnside we came upon a fascinating scene. It was the occasion of the annual blanket washing.

It was a picture such as one might have seen—at least before the introduction of mechanical washing machines —in many parts of the island on a warm summer day.

Near the stream a huge peat fire blazed between flat boulders on which reposed a great pot of water boiling cheerfully. Close by were two tubs in which merry, bare-legged damsels were tramping blankets, and singing snatches of Gaelic love songs as their feet squelched the soap-laden water.

Older women helped, and children played by the stream ; for blanket washing was one of the events of the year. Often two or three families did the work together, the stream providing both water-supply and drainage. When the workers halted for an interval, the whole company sat down to a meal by the river bank. Usually a few young men joined the gathering at this stage, to make the garden party complete.

Beyond Dougal's Loch we continued along the hill road to Kilbeg. Here we rejoined the main highway which curves south past Ostaig House, now the residence of Alisdair MacDonald, grandson and heir to Lord MacDonald.

A mile farther on, we halted at Armadale Castle. Nearby, two men, apparently connected with the castle, were standing. I walked up to them and, stating that I wanted to take some photographs, asked where I should apply for permission.

" I'm in charge here," replied one of them, while the other moved off, " and I can't allow you to take photographs of the castle."

His mouth was one straight line ; his tones were grim. He was apparently one of those peculiar creatures who always feel it their duty to be unpleasant. I was glad to observe that he spoke with a decidedly Lowland accent.

After all, Highlanders may have their faults—not

that I have come across any !—but they are never guilty of unprovoked discourtesy. I did not attempt to reason with the disgruntled hireling. For in this free Scotland of ours it is permissible to wander almost anywhere, even on to the private land of another. All the aggrieved owner can do, is to ask the sheriff to interdict the offending person, and this takes time and costs money.

So I walked leisurely along the avenue to the castle and obtained the photographs I required. As I returned, I passed the honest steward, still mournfully looking after his master's interests. He will no doubt receive a fitting reward—he certainly got none from me.

The straggling village of Ardvasar lies about a mile beyond the castle ; thence a passable road leads past the township of Calgary and on to Tormore. A narrow switch-back road, which even Roddy Cameron was not prepared to venture along, extends to the extreme south of the island.

I had been along this dangerous track on an earlier occasion as a side-car passenger. Mr. Davidson, fishery officer, successor to Mr. Downie whom I have already mentioned, had been presented by the Fishery Board with a motor cycle and side-car. Having occasion to visit a boat-owner at the Point of Sleat, he had recklessly set out in the vehicle of which he had as yet gained little experience in driving.

I went as a sort of ballast. It was also considered safer for two to go together. There was the chance that one might escape injury and return with news of the other's fate.

We passed Aird, an interesting hamlet of white-washed cottages, surrounded by cultivated patches. A number of boats were drawn up on the foreshore, for in

M

Skye most of the crofters are crofter-fishermen. Besides, in the past, particularly before the days of cycling, intercommunication was mainly by sea. For this purpose most of the crofters owned boats, which they also found useful for fishing.

Nowadays all fishing boats must be registered by a Government department, and an annual return has to be made by the owner. Crofters, like most normal people, detest filling up forms. John Rury was no exception, and so the fishery officer had to send him several reminders.

At last a reply came, but not from John. His widow answered, and in reading her reply it should be remembered that although she wrote in English she was probably thinking in Gaelic, a language which has no neuter gender.

Here is her explanation :

" Dear Sir,—I got your letter about the boat, but poor John he died with his stomach in the spring and he now lies rotting on the shore."

That journey to the Point of Sleat was a thrilling experience. We skimmed along the hilly, bumpy road, now skirting some rocky projection by a hair's breadth, again hovering on one wheel over an open ditch, or coming to a sudden dead stop on being unexpectedly confronted by a closed gate.

But we reached our destination, and we returned unscathed. True, there were bits of enamel which never returned ; there were dents on that vehicle which will never be smoothed out ; and there are now several white hairs among Mr. Davidson's black glossy locks which were not there before.

20

PORT-NA-LONG AND DUNVEGAN

MY trip to the south of Skye had whetted my appetite for more, so next day I again set forth with Roddy Cameron. He was waiting on Kyleakin pier as I stepped off the ferry boat, and without delay we were soon bowling along the only road which leads out of the village. Away we sped, through Breakish and Broadford and on past Strollamus.

When I first journeyed along this road in Mr. Skinner's pioneering 'bus, the road had ascended the hill above Dunan. This had been replaced by a new stretch of road built round the shore, again connecting with the old one at Luib. Farther on, it again branched off to avoid the steep climb at Drum-nan-Cleochd.

The road from Kyleakin to Portree had been greatly improved. Blind corners were now non-existent. Bridges had been strengthened, and the whole road resurfaced. The shore road, in addition to being easier for traffic, now served Dunan, a picturesque township hitherto without one.

It was different, however, with the substitute for the Drum-nan-Cleochd road. That road, steep, difficult, and badly surfaced though it was, had nevertheless led up a lovely gorge and penetrated a magnificent glen. Surely it would have been possible to have engineered it so as to make the gradients less difficult.

Here had been a chance for a bright young engineer. Alas, if such ever existed in Skye in our day, he must have been killed in the Great War.

So the Drum-nan-Cleochd road was closed, and a great disfiguring scar marked the site of the new road stretching round the hillside to Sconser. Rising by easy gradients, the road reached a very considerable height near the Moll, where, on a windy day, the motorist would find the gale as great a danger as any ever encountered on that grand old hill road at Drum-nan-Cleochd.

We sped past Sconser and on to Sligachan, where we turned left along Glen Drynoch. In this Glen of Silence we saw an occasional cottage ruin or a straggling sheep. The moors were desolate enough to gladden the heart of the keenest sportsman. There was no " Song of the crofter's boy " to disturb the game.

Along this highway, great flocks of sheep and cattle had been driven to the markets of the south in olden days. Probably for this reason the road had been made comparatively wide. In recent years a rather mean attempt had been made to reduce the width. This has been brought about by resurfacing only the centre portion, and allowing the sides to become grass-grown.

Possibly the road committee is not to blame. Its members may have been tricked into accepting an " increased " Government grant, its award being conditional upon reducing the road width. An astute Government department has been known to " increase " a road grant of fifty per cent. to one of ninety per cent. for a half-width road ; thus saving an ungrateful country five per cent., while at the same time adding to the happiness of our simple councillors.

Glendrynoch Lodge occupies a commanding position at the head of Loch Harport. Here we branched off the main road and proceeded along the south side of the loch for a couple of miles. A cart track on our left led to

Glenbrittle. We turned along this hilly road, reaching the top at a height of 600 feet above sea-level. We descended the other side at a speed which Roddy considered very moderate.

Ahead rose the Cuillins in all their grandeur. On the left, Sgurr-nan-Gillean towered darkly against the sky; on the right, Sgurr Dearg challenged its proud position, while between and beyond stretched a mighty cluster of jagged peaks enclosing the dark waters of Loch Coruisk.

There is a fine stretch of sandy beach where the road ends at the shore. For a number of years this was the calling-place for 'planes flying between Renfrew and the Outer Isles. The most suitable landing ground in Skye, it was probably the most inaccessible by road.

There being no alternative route, we returned by the same rough road to Loch Harport and continued along the loch side to Carbost. There are two places of this name in Skye. We were visiting the one boasting the famous Talisker distillery. The only inn, curiously enough, has no licence.

The road winds up the hillside above the distillery, rising, aptly enough, in cork-screw curves, and continuing its passable but not particularly interesting course to Port-na-Long. We followed it westward to Fiskavaig, a part of Skye where large sheep farms had been broken up into small-holdings.

Here the Board of Agriculture had settled seventy families. They had built a large school; but it was noticeable that even their well-paid optimism had only resulted in the erection of a temporary building.

Many small-holders, I learnt, had been transferred from the Outer Hebrides to this district. Strangely enough, a number of Skye families had been removed from

Skye and settled in holdings on the mainland.   It may be
that the Board of Agriculture, in the course of their
multifarious duties, are carrying out experiments in
eugenics.

The dwelling-houses built by the Board of Agriculture
are more modern, if considerably uglier, than the thatched
cottages which they have superseded.   I asked Roddy if
he approved of providing a bath in every house. Roddy
was openly contemptuous.

"Baths!" he said. " I know a township where there
isn't a house with a bath in it.   Most of the people are
over eighty.   Some of them must be nearly a hundred,
and they never saw a bath.   Yet they look as if they
would have to be shot before they would die off."

We halted at a headland above Fiskavaig Bay where,
across the island of Wiay, we obtained a clear view of
Macleod's Tables.   Farther south, at Idrigill Point, the
Macleod's Maidens were visible.   All around Fiskavaig
were many ideal camping sites.   There was a finely
sheltered sandy shore where bathers could bask in the
warm sunshine.

The Duke and Duchess of York, during their stay at
Dunvegan Castle in 1933, visited this part of the Island,
which is noted for its home-spun tweeds.   A special cloth,
similar to that purchased by Her Royal Highness, is now
known as Port-na-Long tweed.

It was shortly after the Royal visit that Roddy and I
made our tour.   As we returned from Fiskavaig we were
interested to notice that, in front of several houses, chairs
had been placed by the roadside, with a display of home-
knitted hose and homespun tweeds. The passing of our car
had been the signal for householders to bring out their wares.
Even in Skye the business instinct was developing !

Returning to Drynoch, we proceeded along the main highway on the north side of Loch Harport. Stretching inland above Gesto and Struan, this road serves a well-populated district. There were several shops by the wayside, the contents of which appeared to be remarkably varied.

Roddy regaled me with the story of an elderly shopkeeper who had a special system of book-keeping. Not being able to write English, and his assistant being unable to read Gaelic, this old man had evolved a form of shorthand—which has international possibilities—of his own.

Instead of writing down the name of the article sold, he made a sketch, adding the price. Later, his assistant would send the customer a bill, made out in English. One customer, on receiving his account, called to complain.

" Look here," he said, producing the bill, " what do you mean by charging me for a frying-pan ? I never bought one."

The old man was apologetic. " It was a balmoral (Highland bonnet) you got, not a frying-pan." He had put one tail on his sketch instead of two !

Roddy was so pleased with the reception given to his story that he launched forth into an even more—or less —veracious one.

According to Roddy, an elderly Highlander named Donald MacTavish owned a restaurant, very popular with seamen travelling between the Isles and the mainland. Sometimes a large number would have breakfast together. Each one would be asked on arrival to state what he wanted, and in a short time would be supplied.

MacTavish never put the wrong dish in front of a customer, no matter how busy he was, and he always charged correctly on leaving.

It transpired that he kept a piece of chalk in his hand as he received his guests. Then, as each stated his requirements, MacTavish put his hand affectionately on his shoulder, bidding him take a seat. At the same time he quickly chalked a symbol. For fish he put a straight line, for sausages a curved one, and for ham and eggs a circle !

His plan simplified service and obviated mistakes. And when each customer left, a hearty pat on the shoulder cheered him on his way—and removed the chalk !

At the head of Loch Caroy stands the disused Episcopal Church of St. John the Baptist, built less than a century ago, but now fast falling into decay. We halted while I visited it. Roddy remained behind, merely remarking that he only went to church on Sundays.

Crossing the Caroy River, our road penetrated inland, again dipping down to the sea at Dunvegan. Here there is an attractive village with post office and hotel conveniently situated. The harbour, at which passenger and cargo ships call regularly, is nearby. Beyond the village, a tree-lined avenue leads to the Castle, a mile farther on.

Dunvegan Castle, home of the Macleods for seven centuries or more, stands out nobly on its grim rock. In the centuries of its existence it has been added to, altered, modified, and renovated. Its many styles of architecture may provide subject for discussion by experts, but to Skyemen, to clansmen everywhere, Dunvegan Castle is a jewel unsurpassable.

The Castle is open to visitors on Tuesdays and Thursdays, by courtesy of the Chief, Flora, Mrs. MacLeod of MacLeod. Not having chosen one of those days for our visit, we had to pass on without having the pleasure of gazing once again at Flora MacDonald's much-worn stays.

DUNVEGAN CASTLE

There are many other treasures stored in the castle.
A lock of Prince Charles Edward Stuart's hair is contained
in a glass case. There are the Prince's waistcoat and
drinking horn. There is the Fairy Flag, a tattered wisp
of faded silk captured from the Saracens.

Rory Mor's two-handed sword and many other
weapons are to be seen. There is Rory Mor's drinking
cup, capable of holding a quart. There are letters from
Sir Walter Scott, Dr. Johnson, and many others who have
resided there.

In recent years Dr. W. Douglas Simpson, librarian of
Aberdeen University, author of the Official Guide to
Dunvegan Castle, has visited the castle and carried out
extensive research. He has written the descriptive
account of the castle and acted as Club Editor for the
Book of Dunvegan, published by the Third Spalding Club.

The first volume of the Book of Dunvegan, in addition
to Dr. Simpson's admirable description, consists of an
extraordinary mass of papers relating to Crown lands,
charters, returns, receipts, notarial documents, grants,
bonds, contracts, and commissions. There are letters
from kings and other personages.

There are documents which shew that, even in those
days, a Chief was not without financial worries. For there
are household bills, lawyers' bills, and even tailors'
bills.

Seventeenth century prices are interesting. Two
pairs of stockings were knitted for threepence. The
making of a suit cost six shillings, although one for the
laird cost half as much again. The sum of ten shillings
and tenpence was paid for making a coat embellished with
over two hundred gold buttons ! A petticoat could be
produced for sevenpence, but if designed in scarlet with

" ane silver lease and silk," the price rose to two shillings and tenpence.

West of the castle, across Loch Dunvegan, lies the peninsula of Duirinish, with the populous crofting district of Glendale. Returning to the village, we continued to Lonmore where we turned westward, then passing Skinidin and Colbost, reached Glendale.

Half a century earlier, John Macpherson, rebel, " martyr," and humorist, had lived here. In his day there had been too many people for the available land. Many were starving.

Macpherson preached rebellion ; he wanted " living space." It was fortunate for his generation that he had a sense of humour, a gift which was wholly lacking in the continental mountebank who adopted the same slogan not so long ago.

In 1882 the people of Glendale, at the instigation of Macpherson, permitted their cattle and sheep to wander on the farm of Waterstein, even after the bewigged Lords of the Court of Session had strictly forbidden them. Next, these insubordinate crofters actually deforced an officer of the Crown who attempted to serve a writ on them.

The police were outnumbered and failed to do anything. The Government sent a gunboat to the scene. The rights of the lairds must be protected ! John Macpherson, along with three other rebels, Matheson, Morrison, and MacLeod, was taken to Edinburgh, tried by the High Court, and sentenced to two months' imprisonment for breach of interdict and contempt of court.

They were treated as ordinary criminals, and put in prison garb. Morrison and MacLeod had their hair cropped. This was too much for John Macpherson, for a Macpherson wears his hair long ! He reasoned with his jailors. Speaking with that mildness, for which his clan is noted, he expressed sympathy for their pitiful state of ignorance, hinted at possible flaws in their ancestry, and ended by asking them to rectify their mistake.

Higher authorities were consulted. The learned ones of the Scottish Capital discovered that they had committed a serious error, and that this ignorant fanatic from the wilds of Glendale was right ; for the prison regulations provided that those sentenced for contempt of court should be treated differently from common criminals.

Macpherson and his fellow-prisoners were transferred to a large room in the prison, provided with comfortable beds and a good fire. More important still, Macpherson's hair was saved !

North of Glendale lies the township of Boreraig which was at one time held rent free by the MacCrimmons, hereditary pipers of MacLeod of MacLeod. A memorial cairn, unveiled on 2nd August, 1933, now stands there, a prominent landmark.

The inscription, which is in Gaelic, may be translated to read :

THE MEMORIAL CAIRN OF THE MACCRIMMONS OF WHOM TEN GENERATIONS WERE HEREDITARY PIPERS OF MACLEOD, AND WHO WERE RENOWNED AS COMPOSERS, PERFORMERS AND INSTRUCTORS OF THE CLASSICAL MUSIC OF THE BAGPIPE.

NEAR THIS SPOT STOOD THE MACCRIMMON SCHOOL OF MUSIC, 1500-1800.

The MacCrimmons were noted pipers, but Black Lad MacCrimmon is said to have been the greatest of all. How he received his gift of music has been told in Gaelic by the late Rev. Mr. MacDougall, who has stated, " The like of Black Lad never lived in our time or since."

Black Lad appears to have been the Cinderella of his family. His father and brothers were great pipers, but he was not considered worthy to play. One day, when the others were absent, he remained at home as usual to do the work of the croft.

Black Lad's thoughts strayed to the pipes. At last he could resist no longer. He took down the great chanter, fingered it lovingly and began to play.

A fairy appeared and asked, " Which wouldst thou prefer—skill without success, or success without skill ? "

Black Lad replied that he would rather have skill without success.

Thereupon the fairy took a hair from her head and tied it round the chanter, upon which she asked Black Lad to place his fingers. She covered them with her own and commanded him to play.

Black Lad now played as one inspired. No tune was too difficult. The fairy was satisfied. As she was about to depart, she turned to Black Lad and spoke :

" Henceforth thou art the King of Pipers. Thine equal was not before thee, and thine equal shall not be after thee."

Leaving behind the historic places of the west, we now set out to cross to Portree on the east. The road stretches due north to Fairy Bridge, then turns eastward across the peninsula of Vaternish to Edinbane, a prosperous township with post office, school, inn, and hospital.

Continuing along the shore of Loch Greshornish past Borve, we reached the entrance to Lyndale House, a fine old mansion hidden among trees. This was for many years the residence of a sister of Lord MacDonald, and is still owned by a branch of the clan.

During the sixteenth century, Lyndale House was

the scene of a stormy meeting called to decide who was to be tenth Chief of MacLeod. It has been said that the king can make a lord, but that only the Almighty can make a Highland Chief. Anyhow, disputes regarding succession were not uncommon, and the custom of handfasting sometimes complicated the situation.

Handfasting was introduced with a view to ensuring that there would be a direct heir, but too often it led to bitter feud. One Chief would give his daughter to be handfast to another Chief, or son of a Chief, for a year and a day. If before the end of that period there appeared to be likelihood of an heir, the union received the sanction of Holy Church. Otherwise the marital arrangement could be terminated, but such action was liable to create complications.

In the days when marriage was a permanency, the custom of handfasting was probably a convenience. To-day it is hardly necessary, for our marriage laws have acquired a new elasticity. Indeed, handfasting was sometimes regarded as a closer bond than the knot which the politicians now permit our docile, invertebrate ecclesiastics to tie.

Across Loch Snizort there is a fine view of Idrigill Point, above Uig. Out in the loch lie the Ascrib Islands, and looming up on the horizon stretch the hills of Harris.

We followed the moorland road past Bernisdale where there were several picturesque old-world cottages. A little farther on we approached Skeabost House, a stately mansion, beautifully situated, and surrounded by trimly-kept lawns and neat hedges.

Skeabost, formerly the home of a MacDonald, is now owned by Mr. Duncan MacLeod. Even to-day these two great clans, the MacDonalds and MacLeods—in spite of the activities of the Board of Agriculture—still own a great part of Skye.

Duncan MacLeod of Skeabost has been described as a financial genius. Born at the township of Breakish, he early saw there was no prospect of advancement in his native island. Like thousands before him, he left the old home and set out to seek his fortune in the south. He went to Liverpool.

In that great city, this youth, with only a village school education, had to compete with men from public schools and universities. He had little money, but he had native wit and a keen brain. He fought with the giants of finance and won.

When still a comparatively young man, in the early part of this century, he returned to his beloved Skye, a millionaire. He bought the estate of Skeabost, gave liberally to kinsmen, hospitals, and charities, founded bursary endowments and university scholarships.

Below Skeabost Bridge, which spans the River Snizort, lies St. Columba's Isle. On this miniature island there are two roofless churches and an overcrowded churchyard. Two churches on such a tiny islet! Truly a modern touch!

We sped quickly to Portree where, after a brief halt for refuelling, we continued our journey homeward. At Sligachan we rejoined the route by which we had set out earlier in the day.

As we passed Loch Ainort, we noticed two artists' encampments at the head of the loch. Although the light was fading, their sketches were still on their easels.

"Shewing their tweeds," was Roddy Cameron's pawky comment.

21

A TRAIN JOURNEY TO INVERNESS

A morning train leaves Kyle of Lochalsh station at five o'clock during the summer months. It connects with the Stornoway boat, due to arrive an hour earlier, the interval in the time-table being arranged to permit of a delayed crossing caused by bad weather or other circumstances. The train has a good connection at Inverness for those travelling south, London being reached the same evening.

For the east-bound traveller, however, the next train, leaving about six o'clock, provides an equally good connection. It has the further advantage of getting into Inverness after the shops and other places of business are open. It is distressing to reach a town in the early morning, to be one moment diverted from the pavement by a boy with a misdirected hose-pipe, and the next to be the target for the flying refuse from a scavenger's cart.

Hence my reason for travelling by the six o'clock train. It would reach Inverness about ten, by which time the bulk of the inhabitants would be awake. It had rained during the night, and it was still drizzling when I set out ; but by the time Plockton was reached the rain stopped and the clouds began to disperse.

The railway curves round Plockton Bay, and cuts under the castle cliffs below Duncraig Castle, again emerging into the open at Craig. Around the shore curves the railway, at the base of a curiously shaped plateau. Across Loch Carron rise the hills of Kishorn and Applecross.

A glorious panorama now unfolded itself. The clouds had scattered, and the rising sun, peeping over the hill-tops, shed its splendour on the scene. In front lay a beautiful islet, tall pines almost covering its surface. An ideal place for a dwelling-house! No neighbours, no neighbours' hens, no hawkers to leave the garden gate open; in short, an earthly—or rocky—Paradise!

I wished I had brought my camera. It is always the same—I take it with me, carry it for a whole day, and find no occasion to open it. But let me leave it at home, opportunities for its use crop up at every turn. My father's experience with a gun was similar.

He would go for a walk, and rabbits would scamper round him. Pheasants, too, would hop alongside, even sit on the nearest fence and wink at him. But let him carry a gun, they were not to be seen.

As a matter of fact, owing to the strange laws of our country, my father, on whose land the pheasants fed daily, was not legally entitled to shoot one for the sustenance of his family. But his mother tongue being Gaelic, he wisely ignored Game Laws, the provisions of which were couched in an alien tongue.

I find I have wandered away from the railway. And the train was travelling at seventeen miles an hour! However, it has probably waited. After all, what's the everlasting hurry in this modern world?

We jogged along round the shore at the foot of the high cliffs till we reached Stromeferry. The wooden pier, at which steamboats called before the railway was extended, has now been removed. The old stone pier below the station is now used for the ferry which runs regularly—on week days only—to North Strome, half a mile distant. Strome Castle, built to guard the ferry but destroyed over three centuries ago, stands up, a gaunt ruin.

The next halt was at Attadale, a nicely kept platform without much sign of activity. This station serves Attadale deer forest, owned by Captain Schroeder whose residence is nearby. It has neither stationmaster nor other railway employee.

Possibly the people of this district are possessed of a special degree of rectitude, but it seems strange that many more small stations are not operated by non-resident staff. The road transport companies, by halting their vehicles at convenient points and issuing tickets en route, find it possible to run their services with a minimum number of stations and fewer inactive officials.

We sometimes hear complaints about the old carriages put on branch railway lines. Now I am perfectly certain that if any dilapidated old carriage had been put into service on the Kyle line, that is the particular one in which I should have found myself. But no, my compartment was well-cushioned, warm and clean ; and I could go out into the corridor to stretch my legs.

Although the same carriages are probably used regularly on this route, the photographs which adorned the walls of my compartment consisted of Welsh beauty spots with unpronounceable names. To most travellers, and particularly to tourists, a strip map of the district would have been more helpful.

The railway curves eastward round the shore from Attadale. Across Loch Carron may be seen the Sir William Harcourt Hill, so called because its top is supposed to resemble the upturned face of that departed statesman, presumably still gazing across to Skye where, in 1884, he

N

earned notoriety and ridicule by sending gunboats to subdue the poverty-stricken crofters.

The Harcourt Hill was still visible when our train stopped at Strathcarron station. Here there was a tedious delay. A coach containing motor cars had to be shunted into a siding and detached, several motorists having put their cars on the train at Kyle in order to avoid crossing Stromeferry by boat.

Strathcarron station stands at the mouth of a rather dismal glen of the same name. A level road leads to Lochcarron, an irregularly built fishing village on the opposite side of the loch. Farther on, the road stretches to Kishorn, Tornapress, and Shieldaig. From Tornapress a dangerous hill road crosses to Applecross.

We approached the deer forest of Craig-an-Eilan, with Loch Doule in the foreground, and halted at Achnashellach station. Down below could be seen Achnashellach Lodge, for a time the residence of His Highness the Maharajah Gaekwar of Baroda, but now owned by Mrs. Stewart Sandeman.

Continuing slowly eastward, the train passed Loch Scaven, with its two lovely wooded islets, then even more slowly puffed up the steep incline until the summit was reached at a height of 644 feet above sea-level. A mile farther on we approached the southern shore of Loch Gowan and continued along the glen to the River Bran which the railway crosses at Achnasheen.

Achnasheen Hotel is conveniently placed alongside the station, but the traveller who leaves his carriage there for refreshment, will be well advised to take the engine-driver along with him. Failing the driver, the guard may be willing to oblige ; but Mr. Dan Campbell, an engine-driver of many years' experience, tells me it is risky to depend upon the guard. In support of his statement, he tells the following story.

A business man was travelling south from Inverness. It was in the days of the old Highland Railway Company which did not guarantee connections with other railways. He had counted on catching a train at Perth, with half an hour to spare, but now his train was considerably behind scheduled time. He consulted the guard.

" I'll fix it all right," said that worthy, as he pocketed a substantial tip. He then went along to the driver and asked him to put on more speed. That autocrat had other views ; besides, he had seen the passing of the tip.

So it happened that just as the traveller's train approached Perth, he saw the other one disappearing in the distance. He jumped on to the platform, but the guard was too busy to attend to him. The driver, however, listened patiently until he had finished his tale, then commented :

" You oiled the train at the wrong end."

The Achnasheen Hotel has a peculiar distinction. Mr. MacIver, who died recently at an advanced age, was its proprietor at the time of Queen Victoria's visit to Loch Maree. Now Her Majesty, who attended Crathie Parish Church so regularly every Sunday when at Balmoral, was regarded by many Scots people as a strict Sabbatarian. Yet, strangely enough, she chose a Sunday on which to visit Loch Maree.

On reaching Achnasheen her coachman asked for a change of horses. He was promptly refused.

" But they are for the Queen," he pointed out. It was a Royal command. But the Queen had met her match !

" Her Majesty will not be getting any horses from me

on the Sabbath Day," was Mr. MacIver's respectful but firm reply. And she did not !

The train moved along Strath Bran, the well-named Valley of the Drizzle, to Achanalt ; then continuing past Falls of Grudie, crossed the Conon River and halted at Lochluichart. The only interesting fact I can recall about this depressing station is that the stationmaster's triplets —three girls, who probably comprised the entire juvenile population—journeyed daily by this train to school at Dingwall.

Our route lay along the north side of Loch Luichart, a magnificent expanse of water five miles in extent, fleeting glimpses of which were seen from the train. We passed Garve station, where the road branches off to Loch Broom and Ullapool ; then, skirting the southern shore of Loch Garve, crossed the Blackwater, a tumultuous stream rushing along a dark rocky channel.

The Raven's Rock, a dizzy precipice high up on our right, now came into view. Our train moved slowly through the rocky gorge beneath ; then, entering the open again, ran downhill, the battlements of Castle Leod, seat of the Countess of Cromartie, being just visible as we approached Achterneed.

Looking back after leaving the station, we obtained a fine view of the fertile valley of the Peffry. In the distance could be seen Strathpeffer, its church spires and tourist hotels glistening in the morning sunshine. This popular Spa is famed for its sulphur waters, the strongest in the British Isles—a fact of which the casual visitor, who passes the Pump Room at the hour of noon on a sunny day, will not long remain in ignorance.

The railway curves round the outskirts of Dingwall. On a hill above the town the Hector MacDonald Memorial stands out prominently. Across the valley a new Secondary school has been built, the glazed front of its unbeautiful, box-like exterior hopefully facing the south.

Dingwall is the county town of Ross-shire. Here the evildoers come to have justice meted out to them ; here the prison stands waiting. Here the County Council assembles to fix the amount of our rates. Here the licensing bench sits—and decides we are not fit to sell a bottle of medicated wine ! Let us pass on !

Beyond Dingwall the railway stretches through different scenery, wooded pasture land and fertile fields, beautiful but tame after the rugged west. Beauly is the only village of interest on the route. It is nicely situated near the river.

We reached Inverness at last. A haze hung over the Highland capital. The train ran past the station and entered backwards. This is the normal procedure ; it makes one lose the sense of direction. Even when I find my way to the river, I am at a loss to know whether it is running uphill or down.

I have never been able to memorise the names of the streets. They are so short that, by the time I have discovered the name of one, I am walking along the next. Anyhow it is impossible to get lost, the visitor who wanders through the town invariably finding himself back at the station in a short time.

On this particular morning I found everything much as usual. The same figure was leaning against the station entrance, the same postman delivering letters, and I verily believe the same Spaniard selling onions. I wandered past these old friends, for I had business to attend to.

The business of the day occupied the greater part of

a half-hour.   It had been an ordeal, I must confess ; but, in the present state of our civilisation, a necessary one. For my wife had insisted before I left home that it must be done.   She had allowed me no alternative.

So that I might enjoy peace for a little, I entered that torture chamber, and I allowed the miscreant to do as he willed.   Then, physically weak but glowing with a sense of duty nobly done, I crawled across the street to Burnett's Tea Rooms.   And there, refreshed, I realised that my wife had been right—then, as always !—when she had said she would not live with a man whose hair was allowed to grow over his ears.

I had enjoyed the comfort of a compartment to myself on most of the outward journey, passengers usually, after one painful glance in my direction, hurrying off to find a seat elsewhere.   But now, whether due to my newly-trimmed head or for some other reason, I could hardly find space for my long legs.

The carriage racks were filled with packages, boxes and cases were crammed below the seats, and even in the corridor there were strangely-shaped articles wrapped in brown paper.   And still more packages came.   They were brought by message-boys from shops, who called out, " Mrs. MacRae," " Mrs. Mackenzie," and many other names.   These dames responded nobly.

There were handshakes and last goodbyes, and last-minute messages as the train moved slowly out. The return journey had commenced.   The babel changed from English to Gaelic.   I tried to read and dropped off to sleep.

We were an hour late on leaving Dingwall, but even then I did not realise the cause of delay.   At Garve some of the passengers got out, and there was more room to breathe ; but we had passed Achnasheen, the train still far behind scheduled time, before the painful truth dawned upon me. This was the last Saturday of the month !

There may be someone to whom that conveys nothing. Then let him travel by the evening train to Kyle on that day. At every station, friends were meeting the house-wives returning from their monthly shopping visit to Dingwall or Inverness. The train stopped not only at stations but at many intermediate spots—it almost seemed wherever there was a dwelling. Then someone brought a chair and placed it by the side of the train, and in leisurely fashion the passenger descended.

But this was not all. Packages had to be handed down ; frequently the wrong ones were given, and these had to be put back. There had been hours in which to have everything in readiness ; but no, the stopping of the train always came as a complete surprise. Then the leave-takings took time. Guard and engine-driver might fume, but they had to wait.

We halted at lonely shielings and wayside cottages ; we halted, it almost seemed, to let the engine-driver light his pipe. We halted to exchange greetings with a retired octogenarian railwayman, living rent free in one of the Company's houses.

Interesting at first, the continual stopping became monotonous. The novelty had worn off. I was tired and hungry when I arrived home, two hours late. I even felt that my hair, with the passage of time, had begun to grow long again.

22

THE ROAD TO NOWHERE

IT was unfortunate for the parish of Lochalsh that Caesar did not find opportunity to reach it. That great road-maker would not have left it in its present state of isolation. Its unique position is a source of wonder to many who do not know Highland conditions.

Before motor cars came into common use, the roads and footpaths which served for internal communication throughout the parish were probably sufficient. Many places were more readily accessible by sea than by road, for three sides of Lochalsh are surrounded by sea. In the circumstances the ferries at Strome, Dornie, and Kyle provided a pleasant change from the rough jolting over the wild hill roads.

Then motor cars appeared. The roads were actually improved to meet the new conditions, although there are sceptics who dispute the fact. The motorist who resides in Kyle may travel eleven miles by road to Ardelve or Strome. At either place he is confronted with a ferry.

He may, however, penetrate sixteen miles by public road due east to Killilan ; and a further six or eight miles beyond, along a private road into the heart of a deer forest. There the road ends ; for this is the Scottish Highlands,

> " Land of brown heath and shaggy wood,
> Land of the mountain and the flood,
> Land of my sires."

Scott wrote truly when he said, " Land of my sires," but he did not add, " Land of my sons." No, there is no

PLADAIG BAY AND PLOCK OF KYLE

room for our sons in this beautiful land. They are not wanted—except in time of war.

A glance at a road map will shew that the Isle of Skye is moderately well-provided with roads. But what seems remarkable is that there is no proper connecting link between the island and the mainland of Inverness, of which county it forms a part.

Twenty years ago a committee was set up by the Government to enquire into transport problems in the west. This body, called the Rural Transport (Scotland) Committee, 1920, duly issued a report; none of the recommendations of which, it is needless to add, was ever carried out.

It is curious to reflect on how such committees are appointed. Their personnel usually consists of well-meaning elderly gentlemen—we must not call them men—who, having finished their education about the age of twenty, have learnt nothing since.

To them the Great War simply meant a fight, at the end of which the old way of living was to be resumed. They do not recognise the existence of motor transport by road or the possibilities of air travel. No, they turn the blind eye on these " innovations."

So these worthy gentlemen on this particular committee sat down and penned a report—I do not think they would have approved of the use of a typewriter. Their report recommended the building of railways—STEAM railways—through Skye !

But they were not all grandfathers on this Committee. There was one virile member, Mr. G. A. Mackay, whom I knew well. He issued a Memorandum in a Supplementary Report. Here are his words :

" Overland traffic to Skye is discouraged by the fact that it involves two ferries. The mainland ferry might be avoided if a road were made through Glen Cannich from Benula Lodge to Carnoch, at the head of Glen Elchaig. This would involve the construction of only nine miles of new road, and the gradients are not severe."

Glance again at the map. The road which Mr. Mackay recommended would have joined up two existing roads, providing a through route from west to east. It would have brought the Isle of Skye ten miles nearer its county town.

Mr. Mackay's memorandum shared the same fate as the main report. It was duly printed, and supplies were stored in Edinburgh. Any member of the public could purchase a copy for the sum of one shilling. And for this modest sum he could read for himself how the Government had awakened to the needs of the Highlands.

I was enthusiastic about the through road. I interviewed our local Member of Parliament, Mr. Ian Macpherson, on the subject. He was a fellow-clansman, and here a clan counts for more than a political party. He advised me to petition the County Council who would, no doubt, ask for a Government grant, an application which he would support.

In due course a petition was presented to the County Council. That body was not sympathetic. It had been elected to look after the interests of Ross-shire, and it was not prepared to do anything to help Inverness. "Love thy neighbour as thyself" is not the motto of the Ross-shire County Council.

Soon after this set-back, I had a talk with Sir Murdoch MacDonald, M.P. for Inverness-shire. Sir Murdoch, who is a distinguished engineer, was much interested. He suggested that we, in Lochalsh, should ask Parliament to transfer a portion of the County of Ross and Cromarty to Inverness-shire.

" Get the boundaries altered," he said, " The county will look much tidier, and your proposed road will run all the way through Inverness, the county which it will mainly serve."

Sir Murdoch seemed to think it was easier to alter the boundaries of a county than to persuade an unwilling council to build a road. Although I disagreed with this view, I have since come to the conclusion that he was right ; but at the time I pictured the indignation of the Clan Macrae if we dared to suggest the removal of the Five Sisters of Kintail from Ross-shire to Inverness.

It is true that Parliament, in its wisdom, had already enacted the transference of these famous mountains from Kintail to Glenshiel. But that happened in 1726. Now it is more difficult to make progress ; for in these days we are encouraged to make a clamour about real or imaginary grievances. Newspapers are so ready to voice " the free opinions of a democratic people "—sometimes opinions of which their authors are only dimly conscious until they see them in print !

About this time I was elected a Parish Councillor. I have already mentioned how I offered my services on a previous occasion, and I do not suggest that the electorate now shewed any greater degree of intelligence. The plain fact is that there was a shortage of candidates, and consequently I was returned without a contest.

The first duty of the Parish Council was to appoint from each parish or ward a member to represent them on the District Committee of the County Council, and I was chosen to represent Lochalsh. This gave me the opportunity I had sought. I immediately gave notice of a motion to construct a road through the glens, as suggested by Mr. Mackay.

The day of the meeting arrived. The Rev. S. Nicolson, County Councillor, had promised to second my motion, and I felt all the more grateful to him because I had supported his opponent at the poll. I should have mentioned that the District Committee was composed of three non-coherent elements. There were the Lochcarron members on the north of Strome Ferry, the Lochalsh members in the centre, and the representatives of Kintail and Glenshiel from the south side of Dornie Ferry.

There was a full attendance. In addition to my motion, there was one by Mr. Colin Campbell. A County Councillor representing Glenshiel for many years, he had chosen this crucial moment to propose the building of a bridge over Loch Long. He was an experienced tactician, and in support of his motion he had arranged for a deputation of ratepayers to be heard.

The deputation duly appeared, and its various members expounded their views. This was my first experience of the kind, although during my three years' tenure of office I was to enjoy meeting several others. In each case, I may add, they came to oppose some proposal of mine!

I have noticed at these deputations that the spokesmen invariably convinced themselves that they were speaking the simple truth. But why, I could not help wondering, did they always take themselves so seriously?

The principal spokesman in favour of the bridge scheme quoted figures to shew that one sheep and, approximately, the forequarters of another crossed Dornie ferry every three hours. In moving terms he pictured the plight of these innocent sheep being held up owing to bad weather.

So realistic were his words that I could almost visualise the hind legs of some unfortunate animal shivering there on the cold, wet pier. But in case there were any in that meeting too hard-hearted to consider the woes of the sheep, he used a further and more convincing argument. He pointed out that not only did the sheep suffer hardship, but that the delay affected their price at the sales !

There was some discussion after the deputation withdrew, and both motions were put to the vote. The majority favoured the bridge, as, unexpectedly, the Lochcarron members voted for it. Although they did not really want it, they probably thought the scheme so far-fetched that their votes would be harmless. Besides, they were determined in their opposition to a through road to Inverness—which they believed would divert tourist traffic from Lochcarron—and apparently they did not realise that they could oppose both.

The first decision had been taken to build a bridge across Loch Long. The road scheme had been turned down in favour of this fantastic proposal. Nevertheless, accepting the view that half a loaf is better than none, the defeated members resolved to support the bridge proposal, and the vote was made unanimous in its favour.

In due course, engineers visited the scene. Along with them, the members of our committee cruised up the loch inspecting possible sites for the bridge. Afterwards we were entertained to luncheon by our chairman, Mr. C. W. Murray of Lochcarron.

The estimated cost of the proposed bridge was £17,000. Local contributions were promised ; the Government agreed to pay 75 per cent of the cost ; legal and parliamentary formalities were complied with ; but still the bridge failed to materialise. No steps were taken to hustle luke-warm officials, for the Ross-shire County Council—apart from the collection of rates—is not particularly interested in the West Coast.

The years passed. The bridge scheme died of inanition. A new bridge was projected. It was resolved to erect one with an opening span, to allow yachts and other shipping to proceed up the loch. The cost was to be double the original estimate, so the County Council decided upon a toll for motorists. A toll !

Yes, at the present moment, sixty years after the abolition of tolls in Scotland, a toll bridge is actually being built along a public highway of this ancient kingdom. And a toll-house is to be erected.

The bridge will link up the parishes of Lochalsh and Kintail, and will enable the inhabitants of those districts to meet more easily at social functions. Certainly, for local traffic, it will be most useful ; and as a fake museum-piece, it will doubtless attract the attention of antiquarians. But as part of a National road, or even a through road to Skye, it will be an absurdity.

The road beyond Dornie winds steeply up the mountainside in zig-zag fashion, and to widen it would only accentuate the acuteness of the bends. Indeed, so steeply do the mountains slope down to the sea, that any deep cutting would be liable to cause a landslide.

It might be more practicable to engineer a tunnel through the hills. This could also be used as an air-raid shelter, and might be linked up with the disused copper mine in the vicinity of Inverinate. I am told that traces of gold have also been found there, although from my own experience I have not noticed that the precious metal is abnormally plentiful in the district.

Access to Lochalsh and the Isle of Skye by means of a bridge at Dornie is merely tinkering with the problem. The true solution is, definitely, a road through Glen Cannich and Glen Elchaig.

Extend the present road which stretches from Lochalsh to Killilan and the mountain fastness. Extend this Road to Nowhere. Build a connecting road to Benula, only eight or nine miles distant. There are no engineering difficulties.

Even the sporting landowners, in spite of past objections, have come to realise that this road is necessary ; for, not only would it be of service to others, it would benefit themselves. The private roads which are a burden on the lairds to-day would be taken over and maintained by the Government.

By all means let new highways be engineered at a reasonable distance from landowners' residences, so that they may enjoy a moderate amount of seclusion about their homes. But you cannot exclude all but the elect from the most beautiful glens in our country ; you cannot for ever stem all transport across the centre of a county stretching from the North Sea to the Atlantic, to suit the idiosyncracies of one or two self-centred individuals.

Privacy ! The class which talks most of privacy is the class which is eternally washing its dirty linen in public.

Privacy ! It is true that some wealthy men and women come to the Highlands for rest and quiet. Day after day they feast their eyes on the everlasting grandeur of mountain and loch. Week follows week ; the grandeur remains, but the vision fades. You may have a surfeit of scenery, no matter how beautiful or how wonderful ; and there comes a time when even a motor-bus with its plebeian load is a welcome sight.

The proposed road lies along an old right-of-way. In a bygone century, drovers marched through these wild glens, taking with them their cattle and sheep. In more recent times, every legal device has been used to discourage the use of this route. Successive landowners have bridged streams and built smooth roads to replace part of the old track. Nevertheless the right-of-way remains ; and along it anyone, rich or poor, has a right to travel.

There are many such rights-of-way in our country. They are part of our National heritage, handed down to us from the days when lairds and nobles assisted in the government of Scotland ; days when the ancient kingdom was ruled by a king who held his throne by Divine right. They are not privileges won by the eloquence or activities of paid politicians.

23

A LAST LOOK ROUND

THE hour comes to us all when we turn and look back. We think of the time when we might have trod the sunlit heights. Again we peer into the past ; we remember those who lived their lives among us and have now gone from our midst. We remember most gladly those who worked and helped and cheered.

According to legend, there rests in the little graveyard at Killilan the body of St. Filan, an Irish saint who died kneeling before the high altar at Iona and was taken to Killilan for burial. I cannot vouch for the historic accuracy of this interment, but I do know that the body of a saint of a later period lies there.

I was present when the mortal remains of my old friend, the Reverend D. T. Mackay, were laid to rest in this hallowed spot. He was buried at the foot of the high hills, within sound of the roar of the sea he loved.

David Pollock has also gone from us. For many years we saw him on his daily rounds with his black horse and jolting cart. Then he bought a motor lorry. The picturesque gave way to the efficient ; but an engine can never take the place of a horse, and David missed his old friend.

Scions of the nobility have been known to step off the train and greet David as a long-lost brother. Again, on leaving, they have shaken him warmly by the hand— while probably slipping an odd half-crown unobtrusively into a receptive palm. Now he has departed ; but, to quote a classic epitaph, " His son keeps on the business still ! "

I do not intend this to be an obituary chapter, but before I pass on to other matters, I must mention one more departed worthy. He was Mr. Alexander Macrae, better known as " The Pioneer," or simply, " The Pie." Mr. Macrae was in business in Liverpool in his early days; then the call of the mountains brought him back to the Highlands. He lived for some time at Stromeferry ; then, when the railway was extended, he settled in Kyle.

A keen business man, he was a great admirer of Joseph Chamberlain. At the time of the Tariff Reform election, local political feeling ran high and the Pie's effigy was burnt in the street opposite his dwelling. The Pie bore no malice, and the next time one of his opponents

o

asked for goods, I have no doubt he got them on credit as usual !

He read much and held peculiar views on religion. He spoke Gaelic and English fluently, but his knowledge of the Scots tongue was meagre, although I believe he was an authority on " Scotch." He was fond of water, too— in its place—as was evidenced by his bequest of a sum of money to build a bathing pool for the village.

Buildings, like people, pass away ; and their passing, too, is mourned by some. The old Station Hotel, beloved by many who spent holidays there, year after year, has disappeared. In its place there has arisen a larger building called the Lochalsh Hotel. Outwardly its match-box style of architecture is less pleasing to conservative eyes, but the interior comforts make ample amends.

Two new terraces of houses have been erected by the County Council, and these have helped to spread out the population. For some obscure reason, the original houseowners had to build their houses as closely packed together as those of a city slum ; yet the actual value of the land on which they stand, as shewn by the Valuation Roll, is sixpence per acre.

It is not only people and buildings which pass away. The very language of the people is dying. Indeed, to-day, Gaelic has little claim to be regarded as a living tongue.

A society, known as An Comunn Gaidhealach, exists for the preservation of the language. Yet I have known this Society, which holds annual competitions, present a Gaelic choir with a shield inscribed in *English*. Apparently not much hope from this quarter !

Even educated enthusiasts find it impracticable to use the Gaelic language for recording a simple chemical experiment, or in working out a mathematical problem.

We may, for sentimental reasons, deplore its passing, but we have to face facts. In communities remote from towns or villages, there are still some elderly people who speak it ; elsewhere English is the common tongue.

Among recent local improvements, probably the introduction of electric light has been most beneficial. At various times electrical schemes had been brought forward. Mr. Mackenzie, proprietor of the Kyle Hotel, had produced a plan to light the village, in the early days of the Kyle Council.

Next, Mr. John Stewart evolved a hydro-electric scheme for the utilisation of the waters of Loch Ian Oig and Loch Palascaig. Engineers visited the scene and reported on the proposal. They found that the lochs, being near the hilltops, had no rivers flowing into them ; apart from a few small springs they were dependent on rainfall within close proximity. Even in our moist climate there could be no guarantee that sufficient rain would fall during the winter months when it would be most needed, so this scheme, like its predecessor, was abandoned.

The District Council was asked to help. Mr. James Ingram, the energetic District Clerk, took the matter in hand, and the slow-moving County Council were actually persuaded to finance the erection of standards and the distribution of current through the village.

Mr. Douglas Macrae, the local radio and electrical expert, provided the necessary engines and other plant. Now our homes and public buildings have modern lighting, and our streets glow brightly at night, irrespective of moon or almanac.

A motor 'bus now runs twice daily to Plockton, primarily to suit children attending the Higher Grade school there, but also convenient for their elders. Our old friend, Sandy Campbell, no longer runs to Dornie. His race is ended—not that the journey there was much of a race. Now a more efficient motor omnibus carries mails and passengers, and fares are regulated by traffic commissioners.

Among other changes which have occurred, some will probably not be regarded as improvements. The old *Shiela*, which crossed so regularly to and from Stornoway for many years, ran aground near Applecross and became a total wreck. Her successor, the *Lochness*, was built—like the modern hotels—more for comfort than beauty.

The *Lochness* is commanded by Captain MacArthur, a handsome, upright Highlander, equally affable to the fishworker crossing steerage, and the more affluent visitor travelling first class. Notabilities and celebrities who have crossed the Minch on his ship include Lord Leverhulme, Sir Hall Caine, Charles Coborn and Sir Harry Lauder, about whom the Captain has many interesting reminiscences.

The old *Claymore* no longer visits us. Her place was taken by the *Lochgarry*, which duly arrives from Glasgow every ten days during the tourist season. Captain Maclean, her genial Captain, stands on the bridge. It is many years now since the captain, at that time mate on another ship, taught me the intricacies of another " bridge "—a game of which he was also master.

There is one form of transport in which we still lag behind. So far, there has been only one passenger flight from Kyle, which took place some years ago. It was not undertaken by our politicians out of a desire to develop the Highlands. On the contrary, it was entirely due to two young men, Lord Malcolm Douglas Hamilton and Mr. Jack Macleod of Skeabost.

These two air-enthusiasts arrived in the flying-boat, *Cloud of Iona*, which anchored in the bay. A party of ten of us went on board, and were taken up for a short but enjoyable flight.

There are undoubted possibilities for a local flying-boat service. No expensive landing-places would be needed. We have landlocked lochs, calm and smooth in practically all weathers. At present, the holidaymaker from the south loses two days spent in travelling. A brief air flight would take him to our shores without loss of time.

Considerable agitation was necessary before we got a telephone service. In the end it was introduced by the simple, if expensive, expedient of eight subscribers agreeing to pay the maximum rent—for the minimum service—during a period of three years. Now a network of telephones has spread all over the district and through the whole Isle of Skye.

Even the Isle of Soay, lying off Elgol, clamoured for a telephone. The islanders explained that, as it was sometimes too stormy for a boat to cross to Elgol, they were unable to go there to telephone for the Broadford doctor. It might be supposed that it would be equally impossible for the doctor to reach them.

A benevolent Government apparently thought otherwise; that is, if a Government does really think. Anyhow, two wireless stations have been erected, one at Elgol and the other at Soay, both, ostensibly, to enable the people of Soay to telephone for the doctor!

The Brahan Seer has again taken a hand in the destiny of Lochalsh. Three centuries ago he wrote :

" The day will come when the Mackenzies will lose all their possessions in Lochalsh, after which it will fall into the hands of an Englishman, who will be distinguished by great liberality to his people, and lavish expenditure of money. After his death the property will revert to the Mathesons, its original possessors, who will build a castle at Druim-a-Dubh at Balmacara."

The lands of Lochalsh passed from the Mackenzies, as foretold. They were bought by Mr. Lillingston, a generous Englishman whose tombstone is to-day a prominent feature in Lochalsh churchyard. His kinsman, Commander Lillingston, R.N., now owns Lochalsh House, but the greater part of the property was sold at the time of Mr. Lillingston's death.

Sir Alexander Matheson, M.P., a man of great wealth, acquired the estates. He carried out extensive improvements ; he built a road from Plockton to Stromeferry ; he erected Duncraig Castle.

The fulfilling of prophecies was not a fashionable craze of his period ; probably, for this reason, he disregarded the Brahan Seer and built his castle at Craig, opposite Plockton. So, for a time, part of the prophecy remained unfulfilled. Then Sir Alexander died, and later the estates again changed hands.

Within recent years General Sir Torquhil Matheson, K.C.B., C.M.G., after a distinguished army career, has retired to Lochalsh and built a residence. It is situated about two miles from Druim-a-Dubh. Is this the castle which the Seer foretold ?

Perhaps the Seer would not be particular about a mile or two ; like a poet he would be allowed a certain latitude or " margin of error." Prophetic licence being admissible, Sir Torquhil may be regarded as having fulfilled the latter part of the Seer's vision.

Sir Torquhil Matheson now represents Lochalsh on the County Council. He is keenly interested in National Fitness, and in the need for playing fields for the community.

Sports facilities have not been altogether lost sight of, although owing to the rocky nature of the ground, conditions have been difficult. The Kyle Cricket Club uses a small sports field in the centre of the village. The principal matches are those played with the passengers and crew of the S.Y. *Killarney*, a Liverpool passenger ship which calls regularly during the tourist season.

The Football Club is not so fortunate, most of its matches having to be played on larger fields at Plockton or Kyleakin. A Tennis Club flourished for a number of years, but the upkeep of the court was heavy, membership decreased, and the game was discontinued.

Badminton is now popular, the fact that it is played indoors being an advantage in our climate. Monthly tournaments are held during the winter months, and occasional matches are played with neighbouring clubs.

Golf is another attraction ; and certainly the golf course, a nine-hole one, must be one of the finest in the country—for scenery. The approach to it is by a delightful, mile-long walk along a well-planned road. The view, as one proceeds, is marvellous. Down below, in the foreground, is Kyleakin lighthouse perched on a tiny islet ; away beyond, rise the serrated peaks of the Cuillins.

The golf course was a gift from the proprietor, Sir Daniel Hamilton, who bought a large part of Lochalsh some years ago. Since he came to reside at Balmacara, he has done much to improve the amenities of the estate. Tumble-down dwellings have been repaired or rebuilt. He has erected shops at Balmacara and Plockton, both villages formerly served by Kyle ; thus putting into practice the policy of decentralisation of which so many approve in theory.

Sir Daniel Hamilton has done what few other Scottish landowners have attempted to do.   He has opened up the mountains and glens by restoring old hill-roads and constructing many miles of winding tracks, along which everyone is free to roam.   In this respect, and at a time when so many in other parts are discouraging access to the land, he deserves the gratitude of the whole country.

These paths lead to picturesque spots and high view-points from which to admire the distant scene.   One path stretches from Kyle to Balmacara, another branches over the hill to Badicaul, while yet another connects Coillemore with the historic Loch Ach-na-hinich. Twisting and turning, these paths rise to mountain top, stretch over moor, and descend to the shore, disclosing the view of mountain, glen, and trickling stream, revealing the wonder of sea and sky.

Here in Lochalsh, at the Gateway to Skye, although Nature has been sparing in the provision of soil and pasture to bring forth food for the sustenance of man, she has dealt lavishly with the glories of Creation.   Here, in this remote corner of our dear land, is incomparable beauty.

Here is peace passing understanding.

EPILOGUE

Seven years have passed since this record was written, and in the interval many changes have occurred.   Some of the people mentioned in its pages have passed on.   Mr.

NIGHT OVER THE CUILLINS

Melville Wills of Killilan, whom it was a pleasure to meet on our trips to Glomach, has gone. His daughter, Mrs. Douglas, has succeeded to the estate, and it is to her we are now indebted for the privilege of motoring along Glen Elchaig. Glomach has been gifted to the nation.

Balmacara, too, has lost its popular laird. Sir Daniel Hamilton has been succeeded by Lady Hamilton. As a memorial to Sir Daniel, she has handed over Duncraig Castle and the farm of Achnadarroch to Ross-shire Education Committee, to be used as a technical college and training centre. Mr. J. C. Ligertwood, M.A., head-master of Plockton H.G. School, is head of the College, where, at the present time, sixty girls are receiving cultural and domestic training. Later, a number of youths will receive instruction in technical and agricultural subjects.

Plockton has lost two of its ministers, Rev. S. Nicolson and Rev. N. C. Macdonald ; and the Very Rev. Finlay Macrae, who laboured there for many years, has also passed. Sir Ian Macpherson, who represented Ross-shire in Parliament for a quarter of a century, became Baron Strathcarron, but did not live to enjoy the barony very long. Our present member of Parliament is Captain Jack Macleod.

No longer do Miss Mackinnon and Ossian visit us. Others who will not come again include Mr. C. W. Murray of Lochcarron, Mr. Colin Campbell, Mr. Cutcliffe Hyne, Sheriff Trotter ; my brother, Dr. McPherson ; and my old friend, Mr. J. A. Ross.

Some changes have meant improvements. The Dornie Bridge was opened in 1940 as a toll bridge. Recently the road has been classified as a national one, and it is anticipated that the toll will be removed in the near future.

The *Lochgarry*, like many another good ship, rests at the bottom of the sea ; but we hope to see Captain Robert Maclean, D.S.C., cruising among our lochs in the coming summers in command of an even finer vessel.

This record, with all its imperfections, is ended. The wonder is not that I have written it so badly, the marvel to me is that I have written it at all. The reader, in all charity, will bear in mind that age impairs memory, and Celtic environment fosters imagination. Finally, if the course of events has been in any degree misinterpreted, I offer no excuse. I answer in the words of Dr. Samuel Johnson, humbly giving as my sole reason :

" Ignorance, Madam, pure ignorance."

INDEX

200

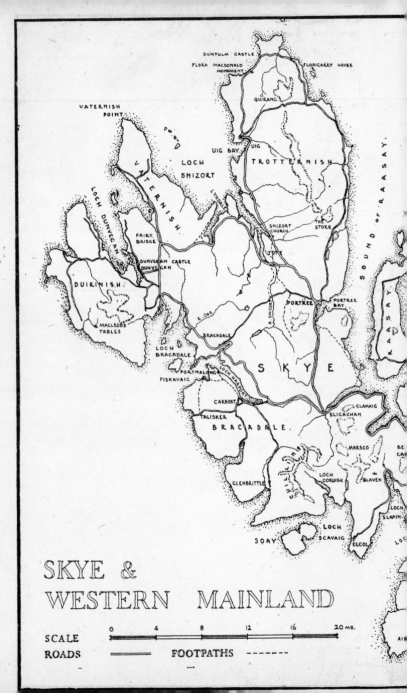

SKYE &
WESTERN MAINLAND

SCALE
ROADS ====   FOOTPATHS ------